Contents

Foreword

History books are often filled with names and dates—words and numbers for students to memorize for a test and forget once they move on to another class. However, what history books should be filled with are great stories because the history of our world is filled with great stories. Love, death, violence, heroism, and betrayal are not just themes found in novels and movie scripts. They are often the driving forces behind major historical events.

When told in a compelling way, fact is often far more interesting—and sometimes far more unbelievable—than fiction. World history is filled with more drama than the best television shows, and all of it really happened. As readers discover the incredible truth behind the triumphs and tragedies that have impacted the world since ancient times, they also come to understand that everything is connected. Historical events do not exist in a vacuum. The stories that shaped world history continue to shape the present and will undoubtedly shape the future.

The titles in this series aim to provide readers with a comprehensive understanding of pivotal events in world history. They are written with a focus on providing readers with multiple perspectives to help them develop an appreciation for the complexity of the study of history. There is no set lens through which history must be viewed, and these titles encourage readers to analyze different viewpoints to understand why a historical figure acted the way they did or why a contemporary scholar wrote what they did about a historical event. In this way, readers are able to sharpen their critical-thinking skills and apply those skills in their history classes. Readers are aided in this pursuit by formally documented quotations and annotated bibliographies, which encourage further research and debate.

Many of these quotations come from carefully selected primary sources, including diaries, public records, and contemporary research and writings. These valuable primary sources help readers hear the voices of those who directly experienced historical events, as well as the voices of biographers and historians who provide a unique perspective on familiar topics. Their voices all help history come alive in a vibrant way.

WORLD HISTORY

SPACE EXPLORATION THROUGHOUT HISTORY
From Telescopes to Tourism

By Jennifer Lombardo

Portions of this book originally appeared in *Space Exploration* by Richard Brownell.

LUCENT
PRESS

Published in 2020 by
Lucent Press, an Imprint of Greenhaven Publishing, LLC
353 3rd Avenue
Suite 255
New York, NY 10010

Designer: Andrea Davison-Bartolotta
Editor: Diane Bailey

Library of Congress Cataloging-in-Publication Data

Names: Lombardo, Jennifer, author.
Title: Space exploration throughout history : from telescopes to tourism /
  Jennifer Lombardo.
Description: New York : Lucent Press, [2020] | Series: World history |
  Includes bibliographical references and index.
Identifiers: LCCN 2018046175 (print) | LCCN 2018048335 (ebook) | ISBN
  9781534567801 (eBook) | ISBN 9781534567795 (pbk. book) | ISBN
  9781534567122 (library bound book)
Subjects: LCSH: Space sciences–History–Juvenile literature. | Space
  flight–History–Juvenile literature. | Astronomy–History–Juvenile
  literature. | Outer space–Exploration–Juvenile literature.
Classification: LCC TL793 (ebook) | LCC TL793 .L6575 2020 (print) | DDC
  629.43/5–dc23
LC record available at https://lccn.loc.gov/2018046175

Printed in the United States of America.

CPSIA compliance information: Batch #BS19KL: For further information contact Greenhaven Publishing LLC, New York, New York at 1-844-317-7404.

Please visit our website, www.greenhavenpublishing.com. For a free color catalog of all our high-quality
books, call toll free 1-844-317-7404 or fax 1-844-317-7405.

As students read the titles in this series, they are provided with clear context in the form of maps, timelines, and informative text. These elements give them the basic facts they need to fully appreciate the high drama that is history.

The study of history is difficult at times—not because of all the information that needs to be memorized, but because of the challenging questions it asks us. How could something as horrible as the Holocaust happen? What are the roots of the struggle for peace in the Middle East? Why are some people reluctant to call themselves feminists? The information presented in each title gives readers the tools they need to confront these questions and participate in the debates they inspire.

As we pore over the stories of events and eras that changed the world, we come to understand a simple truth: No one can escape being a part of history. We are not bystanders; we are active participants in the stories that are being created now and will be written about in history books decades and even centuries from now. The titles in this series help readers gain a deeper appreciation for history and a stronger understanding of the connection between the stories of the past and the stories they are part of right now.

S

Pythagoras realizes
Earth is round by
observing the moon.

Robert Goddard
successfully
launches the first
liquid-fueled rocket
on March 16.

Sputnik is launched into
space by the Soviet Union
on October 4.

Nicolaus Copernicus
publishes *On the Revolutions
of the Heavenly Spheres*.

Galileo invents the most powerful telescope
to date and views things never seen before,
such as a supernova, or exploding star.

NASA is established, replacing the
U.S. National Advisory Committee
for Aeronautics.

Americans Neil Armstrong and Buzz Aldrin become the first people to walk on the moon on July 20.

Yuri Gagarin, from the Soviet Union, becomes the first man in space.

SpaceX's *Falcon Heavy* rocket completes a successful test flight.

The European Space Agency (ESA) is founded.

Soviet Valentina Tereshkova becomes the first woman in space.

The International Space Station (ISS) becomes operational.

THE FINAL FRONTIER

For centuries, humans have been fascinated by space. They wondered about its vast stretches of darkness and the pinpoints of light within it. At first, people could do no more than look at the sky and observe its phenomena, but as scientific knowledge advanced and technology improved, they were able to do much more. By the 20th century, thousands of people were devoting their entire lives to learning about space, and their efforts paid off. In fact, according to the website Mashable, "We have better maps of the surface of Mars than we do of our own ocean floor, and we understand more about the dark side of the moon than ocean life."[1] Today, people have a better understanding of our planet and our place in the greater universe than ever before, but there is still much to learn.

Many early civilizations practiced forms of religion that were influenced by the sun, moon, and stars, but they also applied their observations to more practical pursuits. The ability to make accurate predictions of solar and lunar activity led to the development of systems of timekeeping in ancient societies around the world. The Egyptians and the Mesopotamians created calendars as early as 2000 BC, and around 400 BC the Maya civilization of Central America developed remarkably accurate calendars based on the cycles of the sun, moon, and Venus. This was a great benefit in the ancient world, primarily because it allowed people to predict the seasons, which helped them create crop-planting schedules and aided the invention and practice of agriculture.

The Development of Astronomy

Astronomy—the study of objects outside Earth's atmosphere—is one of the earliest known sciences, going back

For early civilizations, exploring the sky was as easy as looking up. People noted the positions of certain groups of stars, called constellations, and invented stories about them.

at least to the ancient Greeks. Other civilizations that predated or were contemporaries of the Greeks made records and observations of the sky, but Greek astronomers applied logical thinking to their growing body of knowledge and made many determinations that have since been proven scientifically and are now common knowledge.

Many people think ancient civilizations believed Earth was flat, but they actually figured out early on that the planet is spherical. As far as historians can tell, the Greek mathematician Pythagoras was the first person in history to suggest this idea, based on his observations of the moon around 500 BC. He believed it made sense for both Earth and the moon to have similar shapes. A later mathematician named Eratosthenes used geometric calculations in 240 BC to determine the circumference of Earth to be about 28,500 miles (45,866 km), which was very close to its actual circumference of about 24,900 miles (40,073 km). However, other Greek theories, such as Aristotle's belief that Earth was the center of the universe—a theory called the geocentric model—were later proven wrong.

ASTRONOMY VERSUS ASTROLOGY

Astronomy and astrology both involve the study of stars and were influential in ancient civilizations, but in very different ways. While astronomy is the scientific study of space—including the materials that make it up and the movements of the planets and stars—astrology is the use of the stars' positions to interpret the future. The ancient Greeks, Egyptians, Maya, Chinese, and other civilizations used astrology to determine when it was lucky or unlucky to do certain things, such as travel or get married.

Astrology is still practiced today by many people. Horoscopes, which are short predictions based on a person's birthday, can be found on many websites and in some newspapers and magazines. Astrology can be fun and harmless, but it is not a scientific practice. Astronomy, by contrast, uses mathematics, physics, and scientific observations to further understand and draw conclusions about space.

Centuries later, Arab scholars made further scientific strides in what is sometimes called the Golden Age of Arabian Science, which flourished from the 9th to the 13th centuries. Physics is an important part of astronomy, and a Muslim scientist named Abū 'Alī al-Ḥasan ibn al-Haytham (often shortened to Ibn al-Haytham), who was born in Iraq in 956 AD, contributed some of the most important discoveries to this field. He pioneered the scientific method, a precise way of doing research and experiments that is important for getting accurate results. Although he is not often credited, experts such as modern-day physicist Jim Al-Khalili say Ibn al-Haytham's research is the foundation later scientists built upon. In the early 2000s, Al-Khalili reviewed recently discovered work by Ibn al-Haytham that showed he had developed the idea of "celestial mechanics," which explains the orbits of planets and contributed to later work by Europeans.

The cultural and intellectual awakening that took place in Europe during the Renaissance period between the 14th and 17th centuries inspired European scholars to continue the work of the ancient Greeks and Arabs. Nicolaus Copernicus, a Polish astronomer and mathematician, challenged the geocentric model of the solar system. Copernicus spent years developing a heliocentric, or sun-centered, model, but he hesitated to release his findings for fear of being rejected by the scientific community. Fellow scientists eventually encouraged him to publish *On the Revolutions of Heavenly Spheres* in 1543. This book revolutionized the field of astronomy and called into question long-held theories about the nature of the universe.

Other astronomers continued to develop new theories and improve the technology they used to study things in the sky, which are frequently called "celestial bodies" or "celestial objects." The telescope forever changed astronomy by allowing scientists to observe celestial objects in greater detail than previously possible. The Italian scientist Galileo Galilei did not invent the telescope, but he improved it so much that it is generally associated with him, not its previous creators. In 1609, telescopes could only magnify things by a factor of three; that year, Galileo invented one capable of magnifying times twenty. This telescope allowed him "to look at the moon, discover the four satellites [orbiting moons] of Jupiter, observe a supernova [exploding star], verify the phases of Venus, and discover sunspots."[2]

Isaac Newton built upon the work of Ibn al-Haytham, Galileo, Copernicus, and others in his studies of motion and gravity. He published his findings in 1687 in *Mathematical Principles of Natural Philosophy*, which is still considered one of the most important works in the history of science. Newton outlined the laws of motion and of gravitation, which he described as a universal force of nature acting on all celestial objects. His work led to a greater understanding of the universe, but it also raised

Galileo's telescopes were simple by today's standards, but they were impressive compared to past technology.

more questions—ones that could only be answered by leaving Earth. Since then, humans have created spaceships, walked on the moon, sent robots to Mars, and proposed creating colonies in outer space where people could live permanently. Although people have been studying space for a long time, many mysteries remain, and new discoveries are being made every day.

CHAPTER ONE

DISCOVERING THE UNIVERSE

The path of scientific discovery has never been smooth. Mistakes have been made, new discoveries have disproved old beliefs, and even today, key facts remain unknown, creating challenges for researchers. In space exploration, progress has often relied on luck.

Researchers on Earth depend on telescopes, which can capture only the tiniest fraction of what is happening in space. Considering the enormous size of the universe, it is astonishing that astronomers have been lucky enough to have their telescopes pointing in the right direction at the right time to witness celestial events such as supernovae. As Bill Bryson put it in his book *A Short History of Nearly Everything*,

In a typical galaxy, consisting of a hundred billion stars, a supernova will occur on average once every two or three hundred years. Finding a supernova therefore was a bit like standing on the observation platform of the Empire State Building with a telescope and searching windows around Manhattan in the hope of finding, let us say, someone lighting a twenty-first-birthday cake.[3]

Astronomers use star charts, which are essentially maps of the sky, to help them figure out where to point their telescopes to see specific things, such as a planet or a particular star. Early civilizations also drew star charts, but improved technology has made them more accurate. For example, Uranus was first seen by the astronomer John Flamsteed in 1690, but he thought it was a star. It took more than 90 years for astronomers to correctly identify it as a planet. Over time, better construction methods and more powerful optics and lenses improved the capabilities of telescopes. Then, astronomers could discover and observe not only stars and planets, but also smaller formations such as comets and asteroids, as well as the canals and moons of Mars.

The spectroscope, invented by Joseph von Fraunhofer in 1814, received the light given off or absorbed by various objects and broke it down into its specific wavelengths. Since each element in nature has its own unique wavelength, the spectroscope allowed astronomers to determine the chemical composition of stars and planetary atmospheres. This led to the discovery that the sun and other celestial bodies contained many of the same elements found on Earth, although in different states and amounts.

By the beginning of the 20th century, scientists began to feel the need not just to understand the universe, but also to explore it. The field of rocket science was already underway for military purposes. Soon it would be applied to space exploration, shifting the process of discovery in challenging new directions.

CHART 12.

Star charts give astronomers a big-picture view of the sky and help them determine which areas to study.

Math and Physics in Astronomy

Newton's laws of gravitation were still considered the foundation of all succeeding work in the field of physics, but by 1900, they could no longer answer the questions that astronomers and physicists were asking about the nature of the universe. German scientist Albert Einstein was one person searching for a way to figure out how Newton's theories fit with more recent discoveries about electromagnetic fields. Einstein developed his own theories while working as a patent clerk in Switzerland, releasing a series of physics papers in 1905. The most important one among them, "On the Electrodynamics of Moving Bodies," detailed what he called the special theory of relativity.

The special theory of relativity states that the speed of light—186,282 miles/second (299,792 km/second)—is always the same, regardless of the speed of its source or the observer, and that it is impossible to determine an object's movement unless it is compared to another object. Time, on the other hand, is changeable. The faster an object moves in space, the slower time moves for that object.

Einstein published a second and more complex theory, the general theory of relativity, in 1916. This theory focused on the power of gravity, stating that even space itself can be curved or bent by large objects with strong gravitational pulls.

Einstein's work earned him worldwide praise, but his theories revealed something he had not expected. His equations proved the existence of a dynamic—or changing—universe, which opposed the accepted view that the universe existed in a steady

Albert Einstein developed mathematical theories that revolutionized scientists' understanding of the universe.

BLACK HOLES

E instein's 1916 general theory of relativity predicted the existence of black holes, which are "objects of extreme density, with such strong gravitational attraction that even light cannot escape from their grasp if it comes near enough."[1] Their immense gravity bends space itself. However, they were not called black holes until 1967, and the first one was not discovered until 1971. Although researchers knew they might exist, the fact that they suck in light makes them incredibly hard to find. Scientists must identify them by detecting the radiation they give out.

Stellar black holes are created when a large star collapses after burning all its fuel. Supermassive and intermediate black holes also exist, but scientists do not know what causes them. Researchers think intermediate black holes could be formed when multiple stars collide in a chain reaction, similar to dominoes falling, but supermassive black holes remain a mystery. Science fiction books and movies have often suggested that entering a black hole could cause someone to travel through time and space or to a parallel universe or another dimension, but in reality, anyone who fell into one would die.

1.   Nola Taylor Redd, "Black Holes: Facts, Theory & Definition," Space.com, October 19, 2017. www.space.com/15421-black-holes-facts-formation-discovery-sdcmp.html.

state—meaning that it was infinite, stable, and unchanging. Einstein rejected this finding because there was no evidence at the time to support an expanding universe. To make his equation fit with the accepted knowledge of the day, he introduced what he called a "cosmological constant." Journalist John Noble Wilford explained that the cosmological constant represented "an undetected form of energy that was equal to but opposite that of gravity."[4] These two forces supposedly pushed on each other equally, keeping the universe in the same position. Although Einstein added this explanation to his theory, he later regretted the move, since he knew even at the time that it was wrong.

The Big Bang

In 1927, Georges Lemaître, a Belgian astronomer and Catholic priest, used the equations from Einstein's general theory of relativity to prove the case for an expanding universe, ignoring the cosmological constant that Einstein had developed to explain his findings.

He took his work further in 1931 by concluding that if the universe was expanding as time went on, then it must have been progressively smaller in the past, eventually reaching a point when it was so small that it occupied a single point in time and space.

Other scientists reached the same conclusion; for instance, astronomer Edwin Hubble observed galaxies from 1919 to 1929 and noted that over those 10 years, the galaxies grew farther apart. Additionally, he realized that the farther away they were, the faster they moved apart. He figured this out by studying the light stars give off. Each wavelength of light gives off a specific color; stars that are closer to Earth appear to give off light that is closer to the blue end of the spectrum because their light waves are shorter, and stars that are farther away appear to give off red light because their wavelengths are longer. This phenomenon, called the Doppler effect, can also be observed with sound: As an object moves toward a fixed point, the sound waves bunch up, making a sound that is higher pitched. As it moves away from

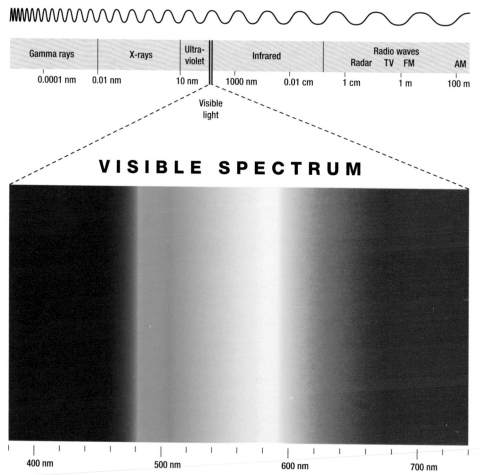

As light waves get longer, they shift toward the red end of the spectrum, as this chart shows. As objects move away from a fixed point, their light waves appear longer. This is why, to observers on Earth, stars that are moving away appear to be shifting toward the red end.

that point, the sound waves stretch out again. Hubble calculated the speed at which stars were shifting toward the red end of the spectrum and came to the same conclusion as Lemaître: The universe was expanding.

Lemaître suggested that some sort of explosion might have caused the universe to expand into what it is today, like a balloon being inflated. However, this inflation theory—more commonly called the Big Bang theory—remained controversial until 1965. That year, two scientists named Arno Penzias and Robert Wilson were trying to test a new way to pick up weak radio signals, but they always encountered interference from background noise. Eventually they realized that the noise came from radiation left over from the Big Bang. About 1 percent of the static on an analog, or non-digital, TV or radio that is not tuned to any particular station is made up of this radiation.

Through further research, scientists came to the conclusion that within fractions of a second after the Big Bang, the universe expanded faster than the speed of light, going from a tiny point to infinite space in less time than it takes to blink. However, one important question remains: What caused the universe to expand like that? Scientists continue to research this mystery, but most accept the Big Bang as the most reasonable theory of the universe's creation, considering evidence such as the cosmic background

AN ALTERNATE THEORY

Although the Big Bang is the leading theory of universal creation, some scientists believe in another, less popular theory. Mike Wall wrote on Space.com,

> This idea holds that our universe didn't emerge from a single point, or anything like it. Rather, it "bounced" into expansion—at a much more sedate [slow] pace than the inflation theory predicts—from a pre-existing universe that had been contracting. If this theory is correct, our universe has likely undergone an endless succession [series] of "bangs" and "crunches."[1]

This cyclic model states that the universe has multiple dimensions, two of which may have collided in the past, causing the universe to start expanding. Researchers are currently looking for evidence that would prove this theory.

1. Mike Wall, "The Big Bang: What Really Happened at Our Universe's Birth?," Space.com, October 21, 2011. www.space.com/13347-big-bang-origins-universe-birth.html.

radiation and the fact that space is still expanding today.

Traveling to the Stars

While physicists debated the origins of the universe, other scientists and engineers focused their work on developing vehicles that could send humans into space. Inspired by the fictional tales of writers such as Jules Verne—who wrote of men traveling to the moon in space capsules that were fired out of a huge gun—these engineers believed that rockets could be built to accomplish what was once considered fantasy.

Rockets as we know them today would not exist without the Chinese, who invented fireworks propelled by gunpowder. Frank Winter, former curator of rockets at the Smithsonian's National Air and Space Museum, researched the field of rocketry and concluded that gunpowder was created by accident around the 12th century, when Chinese alchemists, or early

Research suggests that gunpowder and fireworks originated in China. Modern-day space rockets use different materials, but owe their development to the Chinese.

scientists, were randomly mixing ingredients in an effort to create something that would make them live forever. An article in *Smithsonian* magazine reported, "Centuries of trial and error refined the gunpowder formula, and alchemists likely stumbled upon the property of propulsion."[5] In addition to rocket-like fireworks, the Chinese created rockets that could be used as weapons.

Rocket technology was limited to the military for centuries. However, in 1903, Russian mathematician Konstantin Tsiolkovsky used mathematics and physics to understand rocket dynamics, or how rockets worked. He created a formula, named after him, that remains a key part of rocket engineering today.

Two other scientists—German physicist and engineer Hermann Oberth and American physicist and inventor Robert Goddard—drew conclusions similar to Tsiolkovsky's about rocket dynamics, such as the need for liquid fuel to power interstellar rockets. According to the National Aeronautics and Space Administration (NASA), "There is no evidence that each knew details of the other's work. Therefore, all three of these scientists share the title of Father of Rocketry."[6]

Goddard was the first to build and test a liquid-fueled rocket engine. On March 16, 1926, he successfully launched his rocket near his hometown of Auburn, Massachusetts. The device reached an altitude of 41 feet (12.5 m), covering a horizontal distance of 184 feet (56 m). The whole flight lasted only 2.5 seconds, but it proved that liquid propellants could be used to power rockets—something many people doubted at the time. Goddard's work earned him great respect in the scientific community and became the basis for continued rocket research.

Using Rockets for Research

The U.S. government first began looking into rocket technology shortly after World War II ended in 1945. Several German scientists who had formerly worked on creating rocket weaponry for Adolf Hitler and the Nazi Party were brought to the United States to work with the U.S. Army. The Germans reconstructed the V-2—a 46-foot (14 m) rocket with a range of 200 miles (322 km)—with parts they had brought with them to America.

The first reconstructed V-2 was launched on April 16, 1946, and reached an altitude of 3.4 miles (5.5 km) before tumbling off course and crashing. The team made modifications to the rocket's guidance control and engine, and a second, more successful launch took place on May 10, reaching an altitude of 71 miles (114 km).

Future flights were used for research rather than weapons testing. For example, an October 24, 1946, rocket launch included a camera that took photographs of Earth's surface from an altitude of 65 miles (105 km). Other launches in 1946 and 1947 included instruments to measure solar radiation,

A replica of the V-2 rocket is on display at a German museum.

atmospheric pressure, and composition. One even carried a cargo of fruit flies to test the effects of space radiation on living things.

Around this time, the government of Russia—then called the Union of Soviet Socialist Republics (USSR), or the Soviet Union—was also interested in developing rocket technology. However, the Soviets had fewer resources available to them because many of their factories had been destroyed during the war. Additionally, before the war, Soviet leader Joseph Stalin had ordered the imprisonment and execution of thousands of political opponents, military officials, and members of the scientific community in order to strengthen his hold on power. Many brilliant scientists and engineers who could have aided the rocket program were either dead or in prison, and the Soviets had to build their program almost from scratch.

On May 13, 1946, Stalin signed a decree that formally established a rocket program. Unlike the American program, though, the Soviets were only interested in using the technology for weapons, not scientific exploration. The Americans' fears that the Soviets would try to gain military control of space led to what is now known as the Space Race.

CHAPTER TWO

THE RACE TO THE MOON

In 1947, the United States and the USSR entered a period of political tension known as the Cold War. Both were trying to demonstrate that their country was superior, especially in terms of military power. Neither country trusted the other, and each was concerned the other would attack them if they did not prove they were stronger.

Having advanced technology was one show of strength. At this point, no one had ever been to space, and each country wanted to be the first. The Space Race had started, and as a result, the U.S. space agency NASA was created, paving the way for more discoveries.

Designing a Rocket

In the early 1950s, U.S. and Soviet rocket scientists began to focus on creating more powerful space vehicles. This required them to improve their existing rocket designs in a number of ways because rockets intended to be used as weapons and rockets meant to go to space have very different design requirements. For example, a space rocket needs to be able to hold a lot of fuel—especially if there are people inside it. However, fuel adds weight, so engineers had to consider making the rocket's body out of new materials that were lighter but still strong. New engine designs that provided greater thrust (the force that lifts the rocket) had to be built and tested. More advanced controls for maintaining orientation were needed, as well as systems to better control the rocket in flight.

Both nations maintained a high level of secrecy about their work, and each operated under the assumption that the other was much closer to its goal. In reality, the United States and the Soviet Union were advancing their work at a similar pace, but the culture of fear that the Cold War generated meant that neither side was willing to let up. One of the rocket scientists working for the United States was Wernher von Braun, a German engineer who had designed the V-2 for Hitler but turned to helping the Americans after the war. His participation in the project was controversial because of his association with the Nazis, but the U.S. government was more interested in using his knowledge to beat the Soviets.

In 1954, von Braun called upon the U.S. government to support a satellite program, noting, "It is only logical to assume that other countries could do the same. It would be a blow to U.S. prestige if we did not do it first."[7] Although many people today associate satellites with communications, the word actually describes any object that orbits a planet or star. The earliest satellites did not have the same communications technology that they do today, but they were useful for collecting data and performing other tasks.

President Dwight D. Eisenhower and his senior advisors agreed with von Braun's assessment; however, they chose not to use his rocket for launching a satellite. Even though von Braun's work was more advanced than that of American scientists, the government believed the public would not be happy if the first American satellite to be placed into orbit was designed by a German scientist using a modified Nazi weapon. Instead, they chose Vanguard, a rocket that had been designed by the Navy, to be the first one sent into space to deposit a satellite.

Von Braun, meanwhile, focused on developing the Jupiter rocket, a vehicle with a 1,500-mile (2,414 km) range that was capable of traveling 16,000 miles per hour (25,750 kph). Von Braun and his team developed nose cones for the Jupiter rocket that were able to carry satellites that could be deposited into space. At that point, the rocket would then have to return to Earth, which posed another problem. Objects entering the atmosphere heat up quickly. This is why most meteors that come near Earth do not hit the planet; they approach so fast that they heat the atmosphere around them and burn away. To avoid having this happen to a rocket, the engineers had to make sure the Jupiter's nose cones could withstand the intense heat of atmospheric reentry.

Although von Braun and the other engineers worked directly on the rockets, they relied heavily on people doing calculations behind the scenes. Space exploration depends on accurate math and physics, and in an age before computers, these complicated calculations were all done by hand. They required a team of some of the smartest people in the world. At the time, most of the recognition went to white men, but there were many other people whose work was just as important. One of these was an African American woman named Katherine Johnson, who worked at the National Advisory Committee for Aeronautics (NACA) in the West Area Computing Unit. In the 1950s, NACA was segregated, so black and white employees were kept separate; the people who worked in the West Area Computing Unit were all black women who "analyzed test data and provided mathematical computations that were essential to the success of the early U.S. space program."[8] In 2016, a movie called *Hidden Figures*, about the role Johnson and her fellow black female mathematicians played in the space program, was released.

Katherine Johnson, who celebrated her 100th birthday in August 2018, was a crucial part of the success of America's space program.

With the combined efforts of hundreds of people, on September 20, 1956, the first Jupiter-C, measuring 69 feet (21 m) and weighing 62,800 pounds (28,486 kg), was launched from Cape Canaveral, Florida. This spot was chosen because it is one of the places in the United States that is closest to the equator. This would help the rocket take advantage of the centrifugal force that Earth creates as it spins. This force increases nearer the equator, which makes it easier for the rocket to leave the planet. The rocket reached an altitude of 680 miles (1,094 km), flying at a horizontal range of

THE CONTROVERSIAL HISTORY OF AMERICAN ROCKETS

The American space program relied heavily on Wernher von Braun and his knowledge of rocketry. Without him, it is doubtful the United States would have advanced its space technology as quickly as it did. However, in the excitement over the Americans' eventual achievements, the origins of von Braun's work are frequently overlooked.

Von Braun worked for Adolf Hitler and the Nazi Party during World War II, so his rockets were put together by people who were imprisoned in concentration camps. They were treated as slaves, given no choice about whether or not to work, and they were not paid. Because of the hard work and terrible conditions, more than 20,000 people died while making the V-2. The BBC explained,

> The prisoners – many pulled from other concentration camps for their technical skills such as welding – worked around the clock in an underground factory called Mittelwerk near the Buchenwald concentration camp in central Germany. They lived under appalling conditions, with no daylight, [and] little sleep, food or proper sanitation. Many were executed for attempted sabotage. Eyewitness accounts describe prisoners being hanged from cranes above the rocket assembly lines …

> So would man have landed on the Moon without Hitler's weapon? Probably, but perhaps not as soon. As with so many technological innovations, war hastened the development of the modern rocket and accelerated the space age.[1]

1. Richard Hollingham, "V2: The Nazi Rocket that Launched the Space Age," BBC, September 8, 2014. www.bbc.com/future/story/20140905-the-nazis-space-age-rocket.

3,300 miles (5,311 km). It also carried a 30-pound (13.6 kg) dummy payload. A payload is something that needs to be delivered somewhere else; for example, a satellite taken into space by a rocket and left there is known as the rocket's payload. "Dummy payload" refers to an unimportant object the engineers place on the rocket to account for the weight of a real satellite. This way, they can make the correct calculations so things turn out the same way in the real launch.

"Do you realize what we've done?" von Braun joyfully asked his team after the Jupiter-C launch. "We reached a speed of sixteen thousand miles an hour—higher, farther, and faster than any rocket has flown. If we had just one more small rocket on top, we could have placed a satellite in orbit around the Earth!"[9]

This feat was not overlooked by the Soviets, who had experienced setbacks in their own plans to put a satellite in space in 1956. Their rocket experienced numerous problems during development, and the first rocket that was test launched from the Baikonur Cosmodrome in Kazakhstan on May 15, 1957, blew up less than 2 minutes after liftoff. The second rocket, scheduled for a June launch, never got off the ground, but the third test launch on August 21 was considered a success, even though the dummy payload disintegrated during reentry. The Soviets decided to move forward with their program.

The Results of *Sputnik*

On October 4, 1957, the Soviets launched another rocket containing a simple ball, 23 inches (58 cm) in diameter and weighing 184 pounds (83 kg), with four radio antennae that gathered data about the upper layers of the atmosphere. *Sputnik 1*, the world's first man-made satellite, orbited Earth more than 580 miles (933 km) above the planet's surface.

Western newspapers reported this event with a mixture of wonder and dread. U.S. policymakers and military leaders interpreted the achievement to mean that if the Soviets were capable of putting an object into orbit, they could just as easily launch a nuclear bomb into an American city. The U.S. became more determined than ever to get its own satellite into space.

Sputnik 1 continued transmitting for 22 days before its batteries died, and it burned up in the atmosphere 92 days later, after completing 1,440 orbits. *Sputnik 2* followed on November 3, 1957. The nose cone of this rocket was made bigger to fit Laika, a three-year-old female dog, as well as medical monitoring equipment. Laika died of overheating after 6 hours in the capsule, but the Soviet government kept this information secret for many years, telling the public that Laika had survived until her fourth day in orbit.

U.S. government officials were disturbed by the Soviets' progress. They

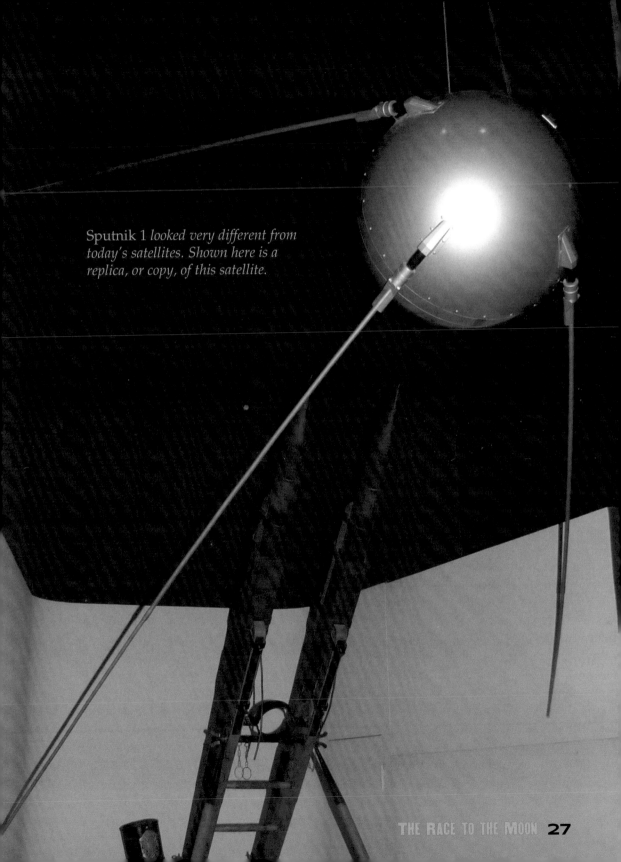

Sputnik 1 *looked very different from today's satellites. Shown here is a replica, or copy, of this satellite.*

approved the test of the Navy's Vanguard rocket, but when the rocket was launched on December 6, 1957, it got only a few feet off the platform before it collapsed and exploded. The rocket's failure was a national embarrassment that increased people's fears that the Soviets were gaining a military advantage over America. U.S. Senate Majority Leader Lyndon B. Johnson, upon hearing the news, warned that same day, "Control of space means control of the world."[10]

The United States soon recovered from this embarrassment, however. Less than two months later, on January 31, 1958, the 30-pound (13.6 kg) *Explorer 1* satellite was launched into space on top of a modified Jupiter rocket. *Explorer 1* contained scientific instruments to measure space temperatures and a cosmic ray counter, developed by space scientist James Van Allen, to measure radiation around Earth. The mission led to the discovery of the Van Allen Radiation Belt, which consists of rings of cosmic radiation that circle high above Earth. These rings have a role in determining how much solar radiation reaches Earth, as well as the amount of electricity in the atmosphere. The satellite continued to transmit data until its battery power ran out on May 23, 1958, but it remained in space for 12 years before falling to Earth. Rocket launches continued to send various scientific instruments into space throughout 1958, ending with America's December 18 launch of the world's first communications satellite, which broadcast a Christmas greeting from President Eisenhower via an onboard tape recorder.

Sending People to Space

The fear caused by the *Sputnik 1* launch prompted Eisenhower to create NASA in July 1958 to focus on the study of flight both inside and outside Earth's atmosphere. NASA, which officially began operation on October 1, absorbed all other U.S. space-related projects in operation at that time.

The agency immediately set about establishing a manned space program, announcing Project Mercury on November 26, 1958. Its goal was to send a spacecraft with people on it to orbit Earth to study the effects of spaceflight on humans and to return them safely to Earth.

To achieve this goal, the agency relied not only on people who worked directly for NASA, but also on a nationwide network of people working at colleges or private companies. These people contributed in areas in which NASA did not have the most current knowledge or expertise. For example, Margaret Hamilton was a software engineer who worked in the 1960s for the Massachusetts Institute of Technology (MIT), which provided computer technology for NASA. Computer science was a brand new field at the time. According to *Encyclopedia Britannica*,

She led a team that was tasked with

developing the software for the guidance and control systems of the in-flight command and lunar modules of the Apollo missions. At the time, no schools taught software engineering, so the team members had to work out any problems on their own. Hamilton herself specifically

Without Margaret Hamilton's computer code—which she wrote entirely by hand, filling dozens of books—it would have been impossible for humans to eventually get to the moon. She is shown here receiving the Presidential Medal of Freedom from President Barack Obama in 2016. This is the highest honor a civilian can be awarded in the United States.

concentrated on software to detect system errors and to recover information in a computer crash.[11]

Scientists confronted a number of technical issues that had to be solved before sending a human into space. One of these was the development of a rocket powerful enough to lift such a heavy payload into orbit. Another was the creation of a capsule that would be large enough to carry one or more people; it would also have to be pressurized, like an airplane cabin is, so the astronauts would not suffocate during the trip. There were other health matters to consider too. Science journalist Deborah Cadbury reported,

The delicate human frame was not designed for cutting through the atmosphere at thousands of miles per hour inside a vast rocket filled with fuel. The rocket's acceleration ... put enormous stress on bone and muscle and could crush vital organs. Extremes of heat and cold could kill. Space, essentially a vacuum with no atmosphere, could cause the astronaut's blood and bodily tissues literally to boil.[12]

In January 1959, NASA publicly announced a search for men capable of handling the mental and physical challenges of space travel. The standards were high: Only military pilots, who at the time were exclusively male, with a college degree were considered for the job. Candidates also had to meet certain physical requirements, including being no taller than 5 feet 11 inches or heavier than 180 pounds (81.6 kg). There was a large response to the call, but the pool of candidates was reduced after a long series of tests that no one had ever experienced before. For example, they had to perform mechanical tasks in rooms that were designed to simulate the environmental conditions—such as extreme heat—that they might encounter in space. They were also given many psychological tests designed to determine their ability to make quick decisions in unpredictable situations and to see how they would handle being separated from most of the human race for several weeks.

While the men were undergoing their tests, a doctor named Randolph Lovelace started giving female civilian pilots the exact same tests at his New Mexico clinic. About 68 percent of the women passed, compared to 56 percent of the men, and the women scored particularly well on the isolation tests.

Lovelace was imagining a future in which people were living in space all the time, and he wanted to see if women could handle space so they could do the jobs they had on Earth at the time, such as being secretaries, telephone operators, and nurses. Essentially, he was looking for women to assist men, not to be leaders themselves. The gender bias was strong throughout NASA, and none of the women involved in Lovelace's tests were chosen to be on the first mission. In fact, it was 20 years before any women would be allowed into space at all.

On April 9, 1959, the seven men chosen by NASA to travel into space were announced to the public as the Mercury astronauts. Called the Mercury Seven, they became instant celebrities and public spokesmen for America's space program.

The Soviets held their own tests for space explorers, whom they called cosmonauts. By the end of 1959, 20 candidates were selected, and a cosmonaut training program was established to prepare them for spaceflight.

In early 1960, the Soviets were ready to begin testing their Vostok rocket. It improved on the previous rocket, which was called the R-7, by adding an additional stage for greater thrust and creating more power. Big engines and a large amount of fuel are necessary to help a rocket overcome gravity and leave the atmosphere, but they also add too much weight to do so. To solve this problem, multistage rockets were developed. These rockets have parts, or "stages," that fall off after being used. This reduces the overall weight that must be propelled into space. Although staging is useful and so far has been necessary, it is complex and can cause complications even if something small goes wrong. For this reason, some researchers are currently working on single-stage rockets, but the technology

Multistage rockets have parts designed to fall off once they have served their purpose. This 3-D illustration shows a satellite separating from a stage of the rocket that brought it into orbit.

is still in its early development.

The first Vostok rocket was launched on May 15 with an unmanned capsule, meaning it had no people in it. The rocket successfully completed 64 orbits but developed an orientation control problem in flight, making it difficult to steer. There were few ways to correct this because most early capsule designs had limited direct flight-control capabilities, such as steering and thrusters. Capsule flights were either controlled from the ground or took the chance that their position would not need to be adjusted in space. Since the Vostok was incorrectly positioned for reentry, it did not pass through the atmosphere but rather bounced off it, much like a stone skimming on a pond. There was not enough fuel to make an adjustment, so the Vostok settled back into orbit, where it remained for several years before finally falling to Earth. The mission was considered a colossal failure because if humans had been inside the capsule, they would have orbited helplessly around Earth until they ran out of oxygen and suffocated.

The problem was corrected, and on August 19, another Vostok flight sent two dogs, Belka and Strelka, into orbit. They returned safely to Earth the next day, becoming the first animals to be successfully launched into and retrieved from space. This impressive achievement of the Soviet program was overshadowed on October 24, when a devastating explosion during final preparations for a test launch of a weapons-carrying rocket claimed nearly 150 lives, including several key scientists and engineers. It took several months to get the program back on schedule.

At the beginning of 1961, NASA scientists were unaware of the Soviets' difficulties. They had overcome a year of mechanical and technical problems that resulted in numerous failed or canceled launches but now felt confident that they were ready to proceed. On January 19, they decided that Alan Shepard, one of the Mercury Seven, would be the first man in space, but more testing was still needed. On January 31, a chimpanzee later known as Ham was launched into orbit from Cape Canaveral. He returned safely and in good health after a 16-minute flight, but von Braun was not entirely satisfied with the mission. Ham's capsule had been partially depressurized during flight, and the capsule returned to Earth more than 100 miles (161 km) off course. Shepard, anxious to be the first man in space, was eager to be on the next scheduled flight on March 24, but von Braun had the final word and called for another test flight.

The Soviet leadership realized that they would have to act fast if they were going to beat the Americans into space. They chose Soviet Air Force pilot Yuri Gagarin to be the country's first cosmonaut to go into space. In the early-morning hours of April 12, 1961, Gagarin was placed into the capsule atop a Vostok rocket at the Baikonur Cosmodrome. Shortly after 9:00 a.m. Moscow time, the rocket lifted off, sending Gagarin into space and into history. Gagarin later recalled his experiences:

> I … felt the giant craft begin to shake all over and slowly, very slowly break away from the launch pad … I felt as if an irresistible force was pushing me harder and harder into my seat … When we got beyond the dense layers of the atmosphere … I could see the far off surface of the Earth … The spacecraft went into orbit—on the broad highway of space.[13]

Several animals were sent into space in the late 1950s and early 1960s to test the conditions for future human travelers. Shown here is a monkey posing with a model of the rocket that took it to space.

A New Goal

The Soviet Union secured its place in history by putting the first human in space, but there were larger goals still to reach. On May 25, President John F. Kennedy raised the stakes during a special message to Congress, stating, "I believe that this nation should commit itself to achieving the goal, before this decade is out, of landing a man on the Moon and returning him safely to the Earth."[14] Kennedy and Vice President Lyndon B. Johnson were both vocal and consistent supporters of the space program because they recognized its benefits for America's defense and its international reputation.

The American space program kept moving forward, achieving longer flight times; astronaut John Glenn became the first American to orbit Earth on February 20, 1962. However, the Soviets were also moving ahead. They sent up *Vostok 3* and *Vostok 4* on August 11 and 12, respectively. This was the first time two manned spacecraft were in orbit together, and they engaged in the first ship-to-ship communications in orbit. On June 16, 1963, the Soviets sent Valentina Tereshkova into orbit for three days; she established another significant milestone by being the first woman in space.

NASA considered Project Mercury operationally complete on June 12, 1963, and scientists and engineers now turned their focus to Project Gemini. Gemini was designed as a series of two-man missions that would test how the human body reacted during longer spaceflights. It would also study technical aspects that would be important to the success of a moon landing, such as the procedures for landing the spacecraft and for reentering Earth's atmosphere. NASA scientists and engineers learned enough during these missions to proceed with Project Apollo, the final series of missions designed to put men on the moon.

The Soviets also started a mission to the moon, although they did not publicly announce it until 1964 because of disagreements over the budget. The first step in the Soviet lunar program was to answer the American Gemini project with *Voskhod*, a spacecraft that had been reconstructed from existing rocket parts. The first two-man crew was sent up on October 12, 1964, and a second mission, during which cosmonaut Alexei Leonov conducted the first spacewalk, followed on March 18, 1965. A spacewalk—also called an EVA, or extravehicular activity—is when an astronaut gets out of their vehicle. Today, this is generally done to test new equipment, set up experiments, and make repairs to satellites or space capsules.

"One Small Step for Man"

The U.S. manned space program had achieved consistently greater success than the Soviet one, due to the Soviets' difficulties with developing a reliable rocket. However, the Soviet Union had completed significantly more unmanned lunar missions, many of which revealed new information. For example, the

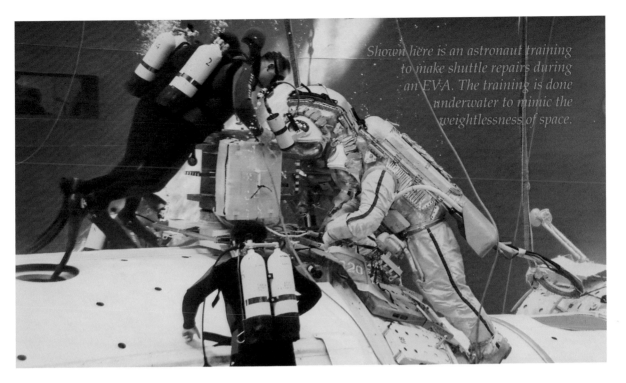

Shown here is an astronaut training to make shuttle repairs during an EVA. The training is done underwater to mimic the weightlessness of space.

Luna 3 probe, launched on October 4, 1959, revealed the dark side of the moon for the first time, sending back 17 images. Later Luna probes throughout the early 1960s succeeded in mapping the lunar surface and maintaining sustained orbits around the moon.

In the United States, by the beginning of 1966, NASA had entered the final stages of development of its complex lunar landing plan. The launch plan called for sending two linked crafts into orbit around the moon. A lunar excursion module (LEM) carrying the astronauts would then land on the moon's surface, while a command/service module (CSM) would remain in orbit awaiting the LEM's return after its mission. Once the astronauts were back on the CSM, it would return to Earth. The LEM was not designed for atmospheric reentry and would remain behind.

Despite several setbacks due to technical problems, the first manned Apollo launch to test the CSM in Earth orbit was scheduled for February 21, 1967. The three-man crew entered the *Apollo 1* capsule on January 27, 1967, to run a series of preflight instrument tests. The test was a full dress rehearsal, with the astronauts suited up and sealed as if they were actually going to be sent into space. Five and a half hours into the test, one of the astronauts reported a fire in the cockpit. Several seconds later, transmissions from the capsule ended suddenly. Ground personnel struggled for several minutes to remove the hatch. Once inside the capsule, they found the interior was completely burned. All three astronauts

BEHIND THE SCENES OF THE APOLLO PROGRAM

A working rocket and a safe space capsule are two critical parts of a space mission. However, few people think about the other important details that must go into it. One of these is nutrition. Even if nothing goes wrong with the launch or reentry, the astronauts will die without food and water. In space, food is not as simple as it is on Earth. Crumbs float in zero-gravity, clogging up important parts of the spacecraft, and food does not last as long as it does on Earth. NASA scientist Rita Rapp worked hard to plan the Apollo astronauts' meals and make the food as tasty and nutritious as she could. She also designed new types of packaging to keep it fresh for the whole journey.

Another important issue is what the astronauts wear. In the vacuum of space, astronauts with no protective clothing would die within seconds from the lack of oxygen and an unpressurized environment. However, they also need to be able to move around and do their jobs. NASA hired seamstresses who came up with a revolutionary idea: They constructed the elbows, knees, and other joints of the suit so they worked like the bendy part of a straw. This kept the astronauts protected while allowing them to move freely. All the suits for the Apollo mission were sewn on regular sewing machines, and the women were so proud of their work that they put their own names inside the suits, the way an artist signs a work of art.

had been killed.

The *Apollo 1* disaster brought the program to a halt for several months while a thorough investigation was conducted into the accident. The final report determined that an electrical spark in the oxygen-rich atmosphere had caused the fire. The report faulted NASA and North American Aviation, the maker of the capsule, for carelessness, sloppy work, and poor quality control. In its rush to keep the launch on schedule, NASA had cut several corners and ignored important issues.

In response, the Apollo spacecraft was redesigned with a new electrical system, fire-resistant materials, and a hatch that could be easily opened from inside the craft in case of an emergency. NASA engineer Chris Kraft wrote, "The Apollo fire was an avoidable tragedy and a necessary catalyst. There was just so much wrong with the spacecraft, the rockets, and our own management that it took a catastrophic incident to wake us up."[15]

The Apollo program was resumed in 1968, and on October 1, it sent up a three-man crew for a ten-day mission to test the newly designed CSM in Earth orbit.

After three successful manned missions in 1968 and early 1969 to test how easily the spacecraft could be steered around the moon, NASA prepared for its lunar landing mission. On July 16, 1969, *Apollo 11* launched Neil Armstrong, Edwin "Buzz" Aldrin, and Michael Collins toward the moon. On July 19, the crew reached lunar orbit and surveyed their landing site in the Sea of Tranquility, which had been chosen based on data from previous unmanned survey missions. There is no water on the surface of the moon, so the Sea of Tranquility is not an actual body of water. It and several other "seas" were named this way because early astronomers, using weaker telescopes than people have today, thought its darker patches were bodies of water. On July 20, the LEM *Eagle*, carrying Armstrong and Aldrin, separated from CSM *Columbia*, where Collins remained. After several tense minutes, *Eagle* touched down on the lunar surface.

Several hours later, Armstrong climbed down the short ladder from

Neil Armstrong and Buzz Aldrin planted the U.S. flag on the moon during their historic 1969 mission. Also shown here is Armstrong's foot touching the moon's surface.

the hatch of the module to the surface of the moon. He placed his left foot onto the powdery surface and spoke into his microphone; his words were broadcast live back to Earth: "That's one small step for man, one giant leap for mankind."[16]

Aldrin joined Armstrong about 20 minutes later, and over the course of the next two and a half hours, they collected about 47 pounds (21 kg) of lunar soil and rock samples and conducted geological and solar experiments.

Before returning to *Eagle* so they could redock with *Columbia*, they planted an American flag and a stainless-steel plaque on the surface near their landing site. The message etched into the plaque read, "Here men from the planet Earth first set foot on the Moon July 1969, a.d. We came in peace for all mankind."[17] Beneath the statement were the signatures of Armstrong, Aldrin, Collins, and U.S. president Richard M. Nixon.

Armstrong, Aldrin, and Collins returned to Earth on July 24 to worldwide

CONSPIRACY THEORIES LIVE ON

One of the first and most famous space conspiracy theories is that the moon landing was faked. Some people believe that in order to win the Space Race, NASA built a set and filmed a version of the moon landing. These people believe it is impossible to land on the moon and cite "evidence" such as the fact that the American flag the astronauts planted in the ground appears to wave in the breeze—even though there is no wind on the moon. The simple explanation for this is that the flag moved as the astronauts moved the pole to secure it in the ground. Other forms of "proof" have similarly simple explanations.

Another idea that has been gaining ground since the early 2000s is the belief that Earth is flat. Related to this is the belief that NASA and other world space programs are fake and exist only to guard the edge of the world—to prevent people from falling off the edge. One "flat-earther" website stated, "In a nutshell, it would logically cost much less to fake a space program than to actually have one, so those in on the Conspiracy profit from the funding NASA and other space agencies receive from the government."[1] Flat-earthers believe satellite photographs showing a round Earth are faked and that no one has ever left the planet. In reality, plenty of evidence proves the opposite. For example, the reason moving objects such as ships seem to appear little by little over the horizon—starting with the sails and moving down, as if they were rising from the ocean—is because they are traveling along the curve of the earth. If the planet were flat, ships would come into view all at once.

1.   Quoted in Natalie Wolchover and Live Science Staff, "Are Flat-Earthers Being Serious?," Live Science, May 30, 2017. www.livescience.com/24310-flat-earth-belief.html.

fame and a planet forever changed by one of the greatest achievements in history. Humans had set foot on, and taken pieces from, a celestial body that had only been seen from afar since the earliest days of the human race. Outer space, previously so unreachable, was now just a few rocket launches away.

Modern-Day Moon Dreams

Ever since the *Apollo 11* astronauts reached the moon, people have seriously thought about working and even living in space. Some presidents and presidential candidates have proposed this as part of their political platforms. For example, in 2012, U.S. presidential candidate Newt Gingrich promised that by his second term in office the United States would have established a permanent moon base. He stated that "the base would be used for 'science, tourism, and manufacturing' and to create a 'robust industry' modeled on the airline business in the 20th century."[18]

Critics noted several problems with Gingrich's promises, primarily the cost. Space programs require huge amounts of money, even for unmanned satellites. The magazine *The Economist* took a closer look at Gingrich's proposal:

Technologically ... it is feasible [possible] to get 15,000 people onto the moon for the kind of money that exists in America's treasury. But then things start to enter the realm of fantasy. Initially most food for the lunar colony would have to be part of regular cargo delivery ... But realistically, it will become necessary to work out how to create a closed-loop ecological system—where everything is recycled, reused and entirely sustainable. Energy must be renewable. Food must be grown, waste water must be reused and the air must be kept clean ...

Even if it were possible to feed, clothe and keep alive 15,000 people, if Moon Base Gingrich (MBG) is not to become the largest federal money suck in history it needs to actually produce something that Earth wants to buy. Something has to be mined, and shipped back to Earth, in an economically viable way. Enthusiasts talk of helium-3 mining and rare-earth metals, but who knows? That's something President Gingrich will want to find out before sending all those people up there.[19]

Many people pointed out that advanced renewable systems were not yet set up even on Earth, so it would likely be extremely difficult to implement them on the moon. Additionally, while some people enthusiastically supported the idea of living on the moon, others felt the money needed to achieve this goal would be better spent solving problems on Earth first. The debate over whether or not a moon base is a good idea continues today.

CHAPTER THREE

UNMANNED MISSIONS AND THE SEARCH FOR LIFE

When Neil Armstrong took his historic first step on the moon, he set the stage for more to follow. By 2019, 12 people had walked on the moon, all from the United States. The various moon missions have brought back more than 800 pounds (400 kg) of moon rocks for researchers to study on Earth. Determining which materials make up these rocks has helped scientists figure out where the moon came from. Previous theories suggested that it was formed out of space dust at the same time Earth originally formed or that it formed somewhere else and ended up captured by Earth's gravity when it wandered too close. However, a study of moon rocks shows that they are very similar to the rocks that are in Earth's mantle—the layer between the top crust and the outer core. This shows scientists that about 4 billion years ago, a moon-sized chunk was knocked out of Earth when an asteroid or other celestial body—probably about the size of Mars—crashed into the planet while it was still forming. Without the Apollo missions, the moon's origin would still be a mystery.

Despite such discoveries, the American public began to wonder what the point of going to the moon so many times was, and NASA struggled with budget limitations, since each mission required building new rockets. The crew of the last moon mission, Apollo 17, returned to Earth on December 19, 1972, and future missions Apollo 18 through Apollo 20 were canceled. Instead, NASA began to develop a more economical, reusable space vehicle to replace the Apollo program. New missions were geared toward near-Earth study and developing unmanned probes to study the other planets. The Soviet Union and other countries also focused less on manned missions and more on sending probes that could take pictures of celestial bodies, as well as test samples of other planets' soil

Along with rocks from the moon, the Apollo 12 crew brought back pictures of Earth, such as this one.

and atmospheres.

Unmanned missions may seem less exciting than manned ones, but they are just as important to researchers. In addition, there are none of the problems that accompany human travel into space. Robots such as rovers and probes do not have nutrition or mental health needs, and they are much cheaper to send than people. However, NASA and other countries' space programs did not give up on manned missions completely. In fact, astronauts from countries all around the world have traveled to space, contributing to humanity's knowledge about the universe.

Probes to Earth's Nearest Neighbors

The first unmanned missions in the solar system focused only on the four planets closest to the sun—Mercury, Venus, Earth, and Mars—and their moons. Astronomers call this the inner solar

The solar system's first four planets are smaller and clustered relatively near the sun, while the outer four planets are much larger and farther away.

system. These planets, which travel in tighter orbits around the sun than those beyond Mars, are relatively similar in size, are made up of solid rocks and metals, and do not have many moons.

The first celestial body to receive the attention of unmanned space probes in the 1960s was Earth's moon because scientists needed data to prepare for future manned missions. Not all of the probes reached their target, but the ones that successfully landed on the moon conducted experiments to study the moon's gravitational field, temperature, and chemical composition. The Ranger probes, which launched from 1961 to 1965, expanded American scientists' knowledge and helped them select future Apollo landing sites. Historian R. Cargill Hall wrote, "Perhaps more than any other flight project, Ranger provided the technologies and the designs for the automatic machines NASA would use for deep space exploration:

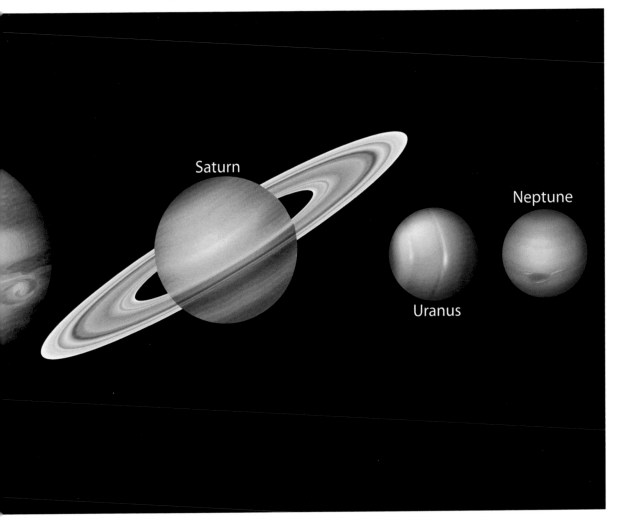

[vehicle orientation] ... onboard computer and sequencer, directional scientific observations."[20]

Probes were also sent to other celestial bodies in the inner solar system. One successful mission was completed by the American *Mariner 2*, which was launched on August 27, 1962. It traveled 180 million miles (290 million km) and flew close to Venus, passing within 22,000 miles (35,406 km) of the planet on December 14. *Mariner 2* was equipped with a variety of sensory equipment that scanned Venus's atmosphere with infrared and microwave radio scopes. It discovered that the planet had a weak magnetic field, surface temperatures higher than 800° F (427° C), and an atmosphere thick with carbon dioxide.

One of the first planets to be explored by probes was Venus.

The Soviet Venera program also focused on Venus during this time. Eleven missions in a row failed before *Venera 4* finally reached Venus's atmosphere on October 18, 1967. The Soviets named the spacecraft *Venera 4* so the rest of the world would think it was their fourth Venus mission, although it was actually their fifteenth. The probe was intended to land on the surface, but Venus's dense atmosphere slowed its descent. The probe's batteries gave out before it could reach the surface, and many scientists believe it was crushed by extreme atmospheric pressure. Before it stopped transmitting data, however, *Venera 4* confirmed the temperature and atmospheric composition information collected by *Mariner 2*. This proved the importance of sending unmanned missions ahead of manned ones. Today, scientists know that the air pressure on Venus is similar to that of being more than 3,000 feet (914 m) deep in the ocean. If humans had tried to land on the surface of Venus, their lungs would have collapsed from the pressure, killing them in less than 10 seconds.

Later Venera expeditions were designed to better withstand atmospheric pressure. *Venera 7* became the first probe to reach the surface of Venus—the first to reach the surface of any other planet, in fact—and transmit data back to Earth on December 15, 1970. The *Venera 9* probe, which reached the surface on October 20, 1975, sent back the first black-and-white photographs.

The final missions with probes *Venera 15* and *Venera 16* reached Venus in October 1983 and succeeded in mapping large portions of the planet's northern hemisphere.

The information from the Venera series was incredibly helpful to scientists. Because Venus is similar in size to Earth, it had been thought for years that there might be life on it. According to the astronomer Carl Sagan, who died in 1996, this belief was strengthened by the fact that the planet was covered in clouds. Before the 1900s, astronomers assumed those clouds were made of water vapor like those on Earth, proving that there was water on the surface of the planet and, therefore, the possibility of plants and other life. Around 1920, experiments with a spectroscope at Mount Wilson Observatory in Los Angeles, California, determined that the clouds contained a lot of carbon dioxide but no water at all, leading researchers to guess that the surface of Venus was full of oil or carbonated water. The debate was not settled until *Venera 7* revealed that under those clouds of carbon dioxide, Venus is just an incredibly hot, bare desert. As Sagan pointed out, "With insufficient data, it is easy to go wrong."[21]

The U.S. Mariner series launched eight more probes before the program ended in 1974. *Mariner 10*, the last in the series, was able to pass by Mercury three times before running out of energy to correct itself when it went off course. It succeeded in mapping nearly half of Mercury's surface, and its instruments determined that the planet had no atmosphere at all and a surface that was similar to Earth's moon.

Investigating the Mysteries of Mars

Some Mariner missions were dedicated to studying Mars. *Mariner 4* was the first probe to fly by the planet, and it returned pictures of a lifeless planet marked with craters. *Mariner 9* became the first spacecraft to orbit another planet after it arrived at Mars on November 14, 1971.

The global mapping conducted by the Mars Mariner missions was used to choose landing sites for the 1975 Viking program. *Viking 1* and *Viking 2*, launched on August 20 and September 9, 1975, each consisted of a probe to study the planet from orbit and a lander to study the planet from the surface. Both reached Mars in the summer of 1976 and uncovered new data. Perhaps most exciting, the orbiters discovered land formations showing that liquid water may have once been present in great amounts on the surface—meaning that it may have supported life. (Frozen water is present in the planet's polar ice caps.)

Mars has continued to be studied with great interest. More than 20 probes have been sent to the planet since 1960, although not all of the missions succeeded. Some lost contact during their flights, while others failed to land—for example, the USSR's 1973 probe *Mars 7* missed the planet entirely and is still orbiting the sun today. However, the ones that succeeded have added greatly to humanity's knowledge about Mars.

There were several probes still active on Mars as of 2019. In some cases, this was unexpected. For example, the *Opportunity*, which launched in 2003 and arrived on Mars in 2004, was only meant to last six months but ended up operating for more than 15 years, making it the longest-running Mars rover. Its sister rover, *Spirit*, which landed three weeks earlier, died after six years because too much dust built up on its solar panels. The dust blocked the light for a full Martian year (687 Earth days), so it could not generate enough power to keep going. In June 2018, the same thing happened to *Opportunity*. It stopped communicating after being trapped in a dust storm for more than two Earth months. Scientists still hoped it would reboot after the storm passed.

Together, *Spirit* and *Opportunity* mapped the surface of the planet and found things such as hematite and sedimentary rock, both of which could only have formed through processes involving water. Polar ice caps had been viewed years ago through telescopes, but the rovers and satellites were able to get more detailed information and confirm that not only had Mars once been covered with water, it is also still present under the ice caps. In

July 2018, images from satellites orbiting the planet showed scientists that there is a span of water 12 miles (19 km) wide and 3 miles (5 km) deep under Mars's southern polar ice cap. They do not know for sure, but they speculate it is kept in liquid form by a salty mixture called brine.

The *Curiosity* rover, launched in 2011 and still active as of 2019, has also found evidence of water once being on Mars, including rocks that were worn smooth by a river long since dried up. Additionally, in June 2018, *Curiosity* found organic matter in Mars soil samples that dated back 3 billion years, as well as the gas methane, which is an organic molecule, in the atmosphere. Although organic matter can exist without life, life cannot exist without organic matter. This gives researchers hope that these traces point to past—or even current—life on the planet. While the general public tends to imagine humanoid aliens with spaceships and advanced technology, space

This 2013 photo taken by Curiosity shows rock formations that scientists believe indicate water reserves on Mars.

LOVE FOR MARS ROVERS

Although the Mars rovers are machines, many people love them as if they were human astronauts. NASA workers, as well as the general public, sometimes look at *Curiosity*, *Spirit*, *Opportunity*, and the other rovers as creatures with emotions. *Opportunity* is nicknamed Oppy, and when it stopped responding to NASA in 2018, NASA tweeted about its status with the hashtag #OppyPhoneHome, a reference to the lovable alien in the 1982 movie *E.T.* One tweet included a link allowing Twitter users to send virtual postcards to the rover with words of encouragement. More than 7,000 postcards were sent—including one from *Curiosity*, which reminded *Opportunity* that *Curiosity* was still on the planet to keep it company.

Curiosity has its own Twitter account with information and pictures of Mars. It became particularly famous on the internet when NASA scientists figured out a way for it to "sing" "Happy Birthday" to itself on the first anniversary of the day it landed on Mars. The rover vibrates at different pitches when it analyzes soil samples, and scientists arranged those different pitches into the song's melody. *Curiosity's* performance only happened once, though. NASA employees want to conserve its energy for scientific research.

researchers would be excited even to find bacteria or some other small, carbon-based life-form.

On November 26, 2018, the *InSight* lander successfully touched down on the surface of Mars, showing that continued exploration of this planet remains a priority for NASA.

The Outer Solar System

The U.S. space program experienced more success when it turned its attention toward the outer solar system. This includes the planets Jupiter, Saturn, Uranus, and Neptune, as well as various comets and the Kuiper Belt, which is a ring of icy debris. Pluto was once considered the last planet at the outer reaches of the solar system but was reclassified as a dwarf planet in 2006.

The outer planets contain 99 percent of all the mass in the solar system, and the smallest among them is at least 14 times the size of Earth. They all have many moons and ring systems because they are so large that their gravity pulls the material around them into their orbits. Additionally, because they are farther from the sun, they are colder, and their ring systems are partially made up of frozen gases that would burn away if they were closer to the sun. Only the rings of Saturn can be seen easily from Earth, however, so no one even

Saturn is the only gas giant whose rings can be seen from Earth. It is so large that 764 Earths could fit inside it.

knew the other planets had rings until unmanned spacecraft were first sent to view them. The outer planets are collectively known as the gas giants because they consist mainly of hydrogen and helium gases, as opposed to the inner planets, which are mainly made of rock.

The United States started sending probes to the outer planets in the 1970s in what was called the Pioneer series. Jet Propulsion Laboratory, a federally funded research facility in California, wanted to take advantage of a rare alignment of the outer planets that would not happen again for 175 years. A long-range probe would be capable of traveling the long distances to these planets by using their gravity to change its speed and direction. Astronomers refer to this technique as a gravitational slingshot. It makes it possible for the probe to use less fuel, making it lighter and faster.

Pioneer 10 remains one of the most famous probes in history. Built in 1970, it featured the most advanced technology available at the time. The instrument package included cosmic ray telescopes and radiation measuring devices, infrared and ultraviolet imaging equipment, and gear for conducting asteroid experiments. It also contained a group of transmitters and receivers to communicate with Earth. The onboard computer was simple by modern standards and did not have much memory, so scientists helped it navigate by performing the calculations themselves and transmitting instructions to the probe.

Launched on March 2, 1972, *Pioneer 10* passed within 81,000 miles (130,357 km) of Jupiter's atmosphere on December 3, 1973. It recorded and transmitted images of the planet and its major moons Ganymede, Europa, and Io. The probe continued its voyage away from Earth, transmitting data of cosmic radiation and the solar wind until, 30 years later in April 2002, its signal became too weak to be received. According to Space.com, "NASA warmly refers to *Pioneer 10* as a 'ghost ship' of the outer solar system as the spacecraft coasts in the general direction of Aldebaran – the eye of the bull in the constellation Taurus."[22] However, if anyone or anything is living in the Aldebaran star system, it will be at least 2 million years before they see *Pioneer 10*.

In fact, the probe was never intended to return to Earth. Carl Sagan, one of the designers of the mission, recognized that it would eventually leave the solar system and travel into deep space. He and another researcher named Frank Drake designed an aluminum plaque and attached it to the probe in case it was ever found by intelligent life on other planets. The plaque contained simple line drawings of a human male and female, and a map detailing the probe's origin on Earth and the sun's relative position in the Milky Way galaxy.

Pioneer 11, launched on April 5, 1973, added to the collection of Jupiter data during its December 2, 1974, flyby, then continued on to Saturn, where it made observations of the moon Titan and discovered two new moons. It passed within 13,000 miles (20,921 km) of the planet on September 1, 1979, mapping Saturn's magnetic field and producing remarkable images of its rings. The last communications were received from *Pioneer 11* in 1995. At that time, it was headed in the direction of the constellation Sagittarius, in the center of the Milky Way. Researchers estimate that it will take about 4 million years for it to get there. Like its sister probe, *Pioneer 10*, it includes a plaque in case anyone ever finds it.

Voyager 1 and *Voyager 2*, launched on September 5 and August 20, 1977, respectively, followed up the Pioneer probes' missions. The Voyager probes contained similar instrument packages, but differed from the Pioneer series in several key ways. For example, they carried more powerful transmitters and nuclear power generators. Probes that fly closer to the sun can use solar panels for power, but the outer solar system is too far away for this to work. The Voyager probes also contained a more detailed interstellar message in the form of a copper phonograph record with a stylus and instructions for how to play it. Sagan explained,

We sent something about our genes, something about our brains, and something about our libraries. ... We included greetings in sixty human tongues, as well as the hellos of the humpback whales. We sent photographs of humans from all over the world. ... There is an hour and

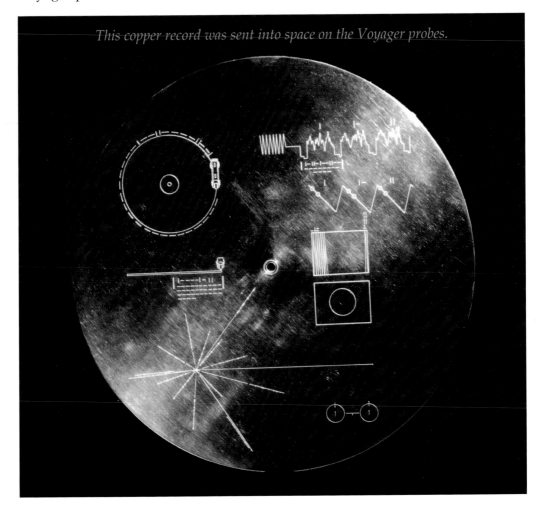

This copper record was sent into space on the Voyager probes.

a half of exquisite [beautiful] music from many cultures. ... And we sent recordings of the sounds that would have been heard on our planet from the earliest days before the origin of life to the evolution of the human species and our most recent ... technology.[23]

The Voyager probes sent back photographs that were the best ones so far. From them, researchers discovered that Jupiter has rings and that the Great Red Spot in the planet's atmosphere, which has been observed for almost two centuries, is a storm more than 12,000 miles

Jupiter's Great Red Spot is a dust storm similar to a hurricane. The planet, which is the largest in the solar system, could fit more than 1,300 Earths inside it.

IMAGES FROM SPACE

Pictures of the planets in books or online are often not actual photographs of the planets. Instead, many are drawings that artists have imagined or 3-D computer graphics. Cameras on spacecraft do not use film. Instead, they have a small device that includes tiny cells called pixels that detect light. A NASA scientist explained,

> When the camera takes a picture, say of Jupiter, each pixel measures the brightness of a tiny part of the scene ... these pixels can translate their measurement of the brightness into a number that is sent to a computer. For example, no light at all could be recorded as a 0, and a very bright light could be recorded as 100 ...

> This kind of data can then be radioed through space to Earth, where the giant antennas of NASA's Deep Space Network receive the signal. Computers on Earth then turn the numbers back into the pixels that make up a picture from space, showing what the spacecraft's camera saw.

> But, now you may be wondering how we get color pictures from space. For each color picture, different pictures are taken through different colored filters. Each colored filter lets through only a certain color of light. For example, a red filter lets through only red light. So the red-filtered pixel data will show the brightness of the red in the picture. If you put together the pixel data from three pictures, one taken through a red filter, one through a blue filter, and one through a green filter, you can recreate the original colors in the scene—and all from shades of gray![1]

1. "If Spacecraft Sent to Other Planets Don't Come Back to Earth, How Do We Get Pictures from Them?," NASA Space Place, accessed on August 28, 2018. spaceplace.nasa.gov/review/dr-marc-technology/spacecraft-pictures.html.

(19,312 km) wide (more than twice the size of Earth). They also learned that there is volcanic activity on the moon Io, and they could see the moon Europa's icy crust in detail that was impossible even with the most advanced telescopes.

As the Voyager probes continued deeper into the solar system, Saturn's upper atmosphere and more of its moons were also closely observed. *Voyager 2* continued past Uranus and Neptune in the late 1980s, discovering Uranus's rings and high levels of methane in Neptune's atmosphere that explained its blue color. As of 2019, the Voyager probes were still transmitting data daily from the outer reaches of the solar system.

NASA continued building and deploying probes to the outer solar system, using the data gathered from these historic missions to design missions geared toward more specific goals. In 1995, the *Galileo* probe became the first spacecraft to orbit Jupiter. It gathered data about the planet's atmosphere and moons that showed scientists that Europa has an ocean under its surface that may be capable of supporting life.

The Cassini-Huygens mission was a joint venture between NASA, the European Space Agency (ESA), and the Italian Space Agency. It featured a craft that orbited Saturn and a probe that landed on Titan on January 14, 2005, the first-ever landing on an outer solar system body. This was its primary mission. After it was completed, the probe started its extended missions, the Equinox and Solstice Missions. For those, *Cassini-Huygens* observed Saturn and its moons for a full seasonal period. In July 2013, it captured a photo of Saturn's rings that showed a tiny Earth in the background. In a campaign to raise awareness about the photo shoot, NASA encouraged Earthlings to step outside and wave at the distant planet. On April 26, 2017, the spacecraft completed history's first ring plane crossing—the "dive through the narrow gap between the planet Saturn and its rings"[24]—and on September 15, 2017, the Cassini-Huygens mission ended as the probe burned up on its descent through Saturn's atmosphere.

The Quest for Intelligent Life

For decades, humans have wondered if they are alone in the universe. Some people believe Earth is the only planet that can support life, especially since the chances of it developing the way it did were very low. Scientists have calculated that if the planet were 5 percent closer to the sun or 15 percent farther away, life would not have developed. Bill Bryson explained,

Venus is only twenty-five million miles closer to the Sun than we are. The Sun's warmth reaches it just two minutes before it touches us. In size and composition, Venus is very like Earth, but the small difference in orbital distance made all the difference to how it turned out. It appears that during the early years of the solar system Venus was only slightly warmer than Earth and probably had oceans. But those few degrees of extra warmth meant that Venus could not hold on to its surface water, with disastrous consequences for its climate.[25]

The evaporation of the water led to the clouds that now surround Venus, trapping heat on the planet and raising the temperature to its extremely high levels.

Other people believe that, considering the size of the universe, there must be at least one other planet where life has arisen, even if it is not in Earth's solar system. As of 2019, NASA has found more than 30 Earth-like planets, which it calls "Goldilocks planets" because they are just the right distance from a sun to potentially support life. However, these planets have only been seen through telescopes; probes would need to be sent to determine whether they support any life. Even if aliens were found living on one of these planets, they may never meet people from Earth. In science fiction stories, aliens attack Earth, perform experiments on people, or sometimes try to reach out peacefully. In reality, the incredibly large size of the universe makes it difficult to even see into the deeper regions of space, much less travel

This is a stereotypical image of an alien, but science fiction creators have come up with more imaginative versions too.

through it. Carl Sagan pointed out that because of the distance between Earth and the nearest potentially inhabited planet, a civilization would have to be at least 1 million years old to evolve intelligent life, create working spaceships, and travel all the way to Earth's solar system.

However, many people—scientists included—have not given up hope of eventually contacting aliens. This is why the Voyager and Pioneer spacecraft included messages, and it is why Frank Drake, one of the men involved in sending those messages, founded the SETI (Search for Extraterrestrial Intelligence) Institute. This organization searches for signs of alien life, such as radio frequencies or laser flashes being sent through space, and attempts to improve the chances of making contact with such beings. As of 2019, SETI has detected several radio frequencies it cannot fully explain. For example, in May 2015, it picked up a strong radio frequency coming from 94 light-years away from Earth. The scientists noted that although it is similar to something they might expect from an alien civilization, it is more likely that it came from a natural event. None of the frequencies SETI has found so far have been detected again, making it impossible to determine what they are.

Unidentified flying objects (UFOs) also raise questions. Some people take reports of UFOs as proof that aliens exist; in 2010 alone, there were 45,000 reported sightings. However, the reliability of UFO sightings is very low. Some people who have made claims of seeing or talking to aliens were later proven to be lying in order to become famous. Others truly believe what they are saying but could be mistaken about

In 1947, an object crash-landed in a field in Roswell, New Mexico. The government identified it as a weather balloon, but rumors started that it was part of an alien spaceship, and the town became famous. Shown here is an exhibit at the International UFO Museum and Research Center in Roswell.

what they saw. Aliens are popular in the media and popular culture, for example, and many people want to believe in them so much that they interpret airplane lights as UFO lights. As of 2019, however, there have been no scientifically proven sightings of aliens or contact with them.

Some researchers suggest that scientists have not yet found aliens because they are too focused on looking for life that is similar to the kinds found on Earth, such as humans or trees. These researchers point out that life may have evolved differently on planets with different atmospheres. For example, those life-forms could be able to absorb carbon dioxide, the way plants do, instead of needing to breathe oxygen like humans. In 2018, researchers at the University of Cadiz in Spain suggested that aliens may even exist without physical bodies. There are no firm answers yet, but the research continues.

CHaPTer Four

FURTHER EXPLORATION

Although it is not yet possible for humans to travel to other planets, there have been researchers working in Earth's orbit for years. In 1971, the Soviets developed the Salyut program to carry out long-term research about the impact of living in space, as well as astronomical and biological experiments. Some missions also conducted military reconnaissance. The Salyut stations were 65 feet (20 m) long, 13 feet (4 m) wide, and weighed 40,000 pounds (18,144 kg). They were launched into orbit unmanned and then followed by crews in separate Soyuz spacecraft who would dock with the station, perform their tasks, and leave a few days or weeks later, after their work was finished.

The Salyut 1 space station was launched into orbit on April 19, 1971. The first crew, sent up on April 23, was unable to dock and returned to Earth. A second crew went up on June 6, successfully docked, and remained on board for 23 days. They performed studies of Earth's weather and atmosphere. The crew returned to Earth on June 30 on a Soyuz capsule, but at some point during reentry, the capsule experienced a loss of cabin pressure, and the three men suffocated before they reached the ground. A few months later, the Salyut station reentered the atmosphere and burned up over the Pacific Ocean.

The United States also designed a space station. Its version, called Skylab, was sent into orbit unmanned atop a Saturn V rocket on May 14, 1973. The solar observatory and scientific workshop was 86 feet (26 m) long, 55 feet (16.8 m) wide, and weighed 170,000 pounds (77,111 kg). Three crews of three people each were sent up separately in Apollo CSMs. The first crew arrived on May 25, remaining on board for 28 days. The second and third crews both stayed longer, and the station logged 171 days of manned operations in total. Nearly 300 scientific and technical experiments were performed, and 127,000 images of the sun and 46,000 of Earth were recorded. Skylab was abandoned after the final crew departed on February 8, 1974. After six years and 34,981 orbits, Skylab fell back to Earth.

The International Space Station

The Soviets used the knowledge they gained from the Salyut program to begin construction of Mir in 1986. Mir was the first space station to be assembled in space, and it used multiple service and living modules designed to interlock with one another. The core module was launched on February 20, 1986, and the first crew boarded on March 15. Scientific and technical experiments continued while six more modules of varying sizes were launched and added to the station over the next 10 years.

Each module carried a unique instrument package geared toward specific experiments related to astronomical observations, the study of Earth's atmosphere and geology, and animal and plant biology. The station, powered by a combination of onboard generators and solar panels, was originally designed to last five years but stayed in orbit for fifteen. Over that time, Mir accepted 137 trips from Earth, accommodating 104 different people from 12 nations. The vast majority of them came from Russia and the United States.

Life on the space station became increasingly difficult in later years. Mir showed signs of damage as it aged, such as electrical and equipment problems. In addition, funding was difficult to come by after the political collapse of the Soviet Union in 1991 (when the country once again became

Recent research has revealed that the countries highlighted on this map are capable of launching objects into orbit around Earth.

known as Russia), and the program was suspended after its last crew returned to Earth on August 28, 1999. In October 2000, the Russians decided to take the station out of orbit, and it broke up over the South Pacific Ocean on March 23, 2001.

Mir's cancellation allowed Russia to join the U.S., European, Canadian, and Japanese space agencies in the construction of the International Space Station (ISS), which began on November 20, 1998. The ISS was assembled in the same fashion as Mir, with several nations adding modules and components that were carried into orbit by U.S. and Russian vehicles. When construction was completed in 2012, the ISS was larger than a football field, with a mass of 440 tons (400 mt). Inside, the living and working space for the astronauts was about the size of a five-bedroom house.

The first resident crew arrived on November 2, 2000, and the station has been inhabited ever since. Although people from many countries have lived and worked on the ISS, it is mainly controlled by Russians and Americans. *The Atlantic* magazine explained, "Operations on the ISS are split in half, with one side run by Americans and the other by the Russians. (This doesn't prevent them from hanging out, of course; they spend plenty of time together, and are trained to speak both English and Russian.)"[26] NASA schedules free time for its astronauts, allowing them to play games, read books, or simply look out the window at the beauty of space.

In addition to spending time together relaxing, teams from both countries perform certain tasks together. However, because two separate leaders might disagree with each other, there is only one commander of the ISS, to whom all the other crew members report. In 2008, Peggy Whitson made history by becoming the first female ISS commander. She set other records too: She was both the first female and first non-military chief of the astronaut corps, and as of 2018, when she retired, she held the record for the most time spent in space by any American, as well as the most spacewalks performed by a woman— 10 in all.

The main purpose of the ISS is to provide a place for scientists to carry out experiments that require a weightless environment and therefore cannot be done on Earth. For example, by removing the effects of gravity, researchers have learned more about other factors that affect the way plants grow. This can not only teach people about life on Earth, but it can also help astronauts learn how to grow their own food in space for future long-term missions. Another study revealed that zero-gravity causes some bacteria to develop in ways that make them stronger and more deadly. Knowing that information, researchers can adjust conditions to potentially make certain diseases less dangerous.

Even the astronauts themselves are a type of experiment, since the effects of weightlessness can teach researchers a lot about the human body. According to *Popular Science* magazine,

> The body's natural ability to reabsorb calcium into the bones doesn't function in zero-G. So in space we lose bone density at a rate ten times faster than osteoporosis [bone disease]. Muscles also atrophy [weaken] because you're not using them much: you can get anywhere with a tiny push. For both reasons, you need to exercise a couple hours a day.[27]

Other body systems also relax when gravity is removed. This causes effects such as a loss of orientation (difficulty telling which way is up or down) and a disruption in the body's ability to tell exactly where limbs are relative to the rest of the body. For instance, on Earth, someone who sticks their arm out knows they are doing this because it soon starts to ache with the effort of holding it up. In zero-gravity, with no pressure on their limbs, astronauts can lose track of where their arms and legs are.

Another medical issue that remained a mystery to NASA researchers for many years was the effects on astronauts' eyes. As many as two-thirds of astronauts have reported their eyesight getting worse, even after returning to Earth. In 2016, a research team from the University of Miami in Florida announced that the problem was caused by a buildup of cerebrospinal fluid (CSF) in the skull, particularly at the back of the eyes. This fluid cushions the brain and spinal cord. On Earth, the amount of fluid in certain parts of the body changes depending on whether a person is sitting, lying down, or standing up. In space, CSF cannot adjust to the body's changing positions as well, so it builds up and puts pressure on the eyes, damaging eyesight. Astronaut Scott Kelly, for example, had excellent eyesight before he spent a year in space. When he returned to Earth, he had to wear reading glasses.

According to scientists, humans will not be able to undertake longer space journeys—including manned missions to Mars—until this problem is solved. As of early 2019, the longest time any person had spent in space was 438 days. This record was set by Russian cosmonaut Valeri Polyakov aboard the Mir space station from 1994 to 1995. Most people do not spend more than 6 months on the ISS, but it would take at least 18 months for a crew to reach Mars. Considering how much people's eyesight can deteriorate after only six months to a year, a trip of that length carries a high risk of causing permanent blindness to crew members.

Although medical problems such as these are of great concern to NASA and other countries' space programs, even helping astronauts go through their daily routines can be a challenge. Weightlessness affects activities as simple as eating or going to the bathroom. For example, on Earth, gravity causes

SCOTT KELLY'S YEAR IN SPACE

From 2015 to 2016, astronaut Scott Kelly and his twin brother Mark were part of an important study. Identical twins such as the Kelly brothers have the same DNA, which controls genes that pass hereditary information from parents to children. When certain genes turn "on" or "off"—a process known as gene expression—it affects how a person's body reacts to the environment around it. Studies with twins are useful to determine how different environmental factors can affect a person's genes. For the Kelly study, Scott spent a year in space while Mark remained on Earth. By comparing the two brothers before and after, researchers gained a better understanding of how space affects a person.

The twin study revealed some changes in Scott's gene expression, caused by factors such as decreased oxygen and changes in nutrition. These genes affected things such as the immune system (which helps the body fight off disease), how the body repairs damaged DNA, and bone formation. Most of Scott's genes returned to the way they had been once he returned to Earth; only 7 percent remained changed after 6 months back on the ground.

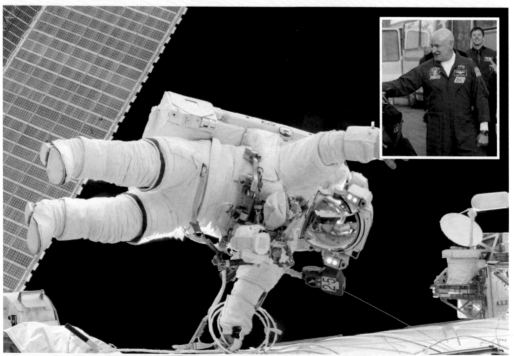

Scott Kelly is shown here approaching the launch pad in advance of his year in space and completing tasks on the outside of the space station during a spacewalk.

urine to put pressure on a person's bladder as it fills. Without gravity, there is no pressure, so sometimes astronauts cannot tell when they have to go to the bathroom. For this reason, they must sometimes wear adult diapers—for example, when they are doing a spacewalk and cannot quickly get to a toilet. When they do use the toilet, they must hang onto a strap to prevent themselves from floating off before they are done.

Conserving water is an important concern on the ISS because astronauts cannot simply turn on a faucet or go to the store for a bottle of water. For this reason, all liquid—including sweat and urine—is collected, recycled, and cleaned so that it can be used again for drinking and bathing. Doing laundry is not an option, so astronauts generally wear their clothes for longer than they would on Earth. When they are ready to return to Earth, they place all their dirty clothes and other garbage in a one-time-use spacecraft that is launched separately and burns up in the atmosphere. Seen from the ground, this would look like a shooting star.

Showering can be tricky because in zero-gravity, the water droplets float around instead of falling straight down as they do on Earth. To address this, astronauts use pouches filled with liquid soap and water that they can squeeze directly onto their skin and use rinseless shampoo for their hair. They dry

Being weightless seems like fun, but living in zero-gravity presents unique challenges.

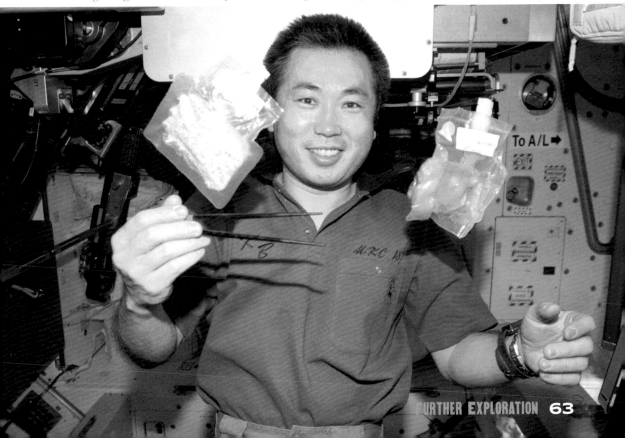

off with a towel, and anything left evaporates through the spacecraft's airflow system.

When it is time to go to sleep on the ISS, the astronauts must attach their sleeping bags to the wall or ceiling so they do not float around the room. Getting the right amount of sleep can be difficult because every 24 hours, the astronauts experience 16 sunrises and sunsets. This makes it hard for their bodies to tell when they should be awake or asleep. To get around this problem, instead of relying on a sunrise to tell them when a new day has started, they wear eyeshades or keep the windows covered to keep out the sun and then use an alarm clock set for 8 hours later.

These solutions to the difficulties of life in space have been developed through trial and error over time. The first people in space did not know exactly what to expect, and sometimes equipment had to be redesigned when unforeseen problems came up. For instance, when Alan Shepard went to space in 1961, he had to wait for 5 hours before liftoff. He could not take his suit off to go to the bathroom, so he had to urinate inside it. The liquid made his heart monitor short-circuit. The suit was redesigned with a bag in it so that when John Glenn went to space in 1962, he could urinate and then dispose of the waste later. Later, NASA developed high-tech adult diapers that absorb and store urine so it can later be cleaned and recycled into drinking water.

The Space Shuttle Program

Much of the work aboard the International Space Station was made possible by the space shuttle. This spacecraft was designed by NASA to launch like a rocket, land like a conventional airplane, and be reusable for multiple missions. The space agency began developing the shuttle in January 1972 as a replacement for the Apollo program. NASA engineers debated various concepts before settling on a craft that contained a large space for its payload and could operate effectively under its own power while in orbit. The agency finally settled on a design for a 4.5-million-pound (2 million kg) craft that required two solid rocket boosters and a large external fuel tank for liftoff, all of which would detach and drop off by the time the shuttle reached orbit.

The first shuttle, *Enterprise*, was unveiled on September 17, 1976. It was not built for space travel but was used to conduct test flights and landings to get astronauts used to the way it would feel. The first fully functional shuttle, *Columbia*, was completed in March 1979 and was launched into space on April 12, 1981. The mission lasted two days and brought America's six-year interruption from manned spaceflight to an end. It was considered a complete success.

Five shuttles were built over the course of the 30-year program; all were named after famous science and exploration vessels. *Challenger* flew for the first time in 1983, and on its fifth mission that same year, it carried Sally Ride, the first American woman in space. This was a historic event because even then, NASA was still mostly male-dominated. Ride and her five female coworkers proved to NASA and the rest of the world that women were just as good as men at being astronauts and scientists. These female astronauts were an inspiration to others, including Mae Jemison, who became the first black woman in space in 1992.

The *Discovery* shuttle was launched in 1984, followed by Atlantis in 1985. The shuttle program suffered a disaster in 1986, when *Challenger* exploded shortly after liftoff, killing its seven crew members. *Endeavor* was added in 1992 to replace *Challenger*. The American shuttle program continued for almost another 20 years—although not without more setbacks and tragedy—but was permanently retired in 2011 in order to free up money and resources to pursue other types of manned missions, including possible journeys to Mars. Today, the only way for astronauts to get to the

Mae Jemison, an astronaut and a doctor, made history when she became the first black woman in space. She also appeared in an episode of the science fiction show Star Trek: The Next Generation.

SO YOU WANT TO BE AN ASTRONAUT

Becoming an astronaut may seem like an impossible dream, but some people are able to achieve it through hard work and dedication. When NASA's space program first started, candidates were restricted to white men who had been in the military, but today, anyone who meets the requirements can be considered. According to NASA,

> For mission specialists and pilot astronauts, the minimum requirements include a bachelor's degree in engineering, science or mathematics ... Three years of related experience must follow the degree, and an advanced degree is desirable. Pilot astronauts must have at least 1,000 hours of experience in jet aircraft, and they need better vision than mission specialists.[1]

Top grades and excellent physical health are necessary to beat out the competition. Every two years, about 4,000 people apply for only 20 openings.

1. "NASA—Astronauts," NASA, accessed on September 12, 2018. www.nasa.gov/centers/kennedy/about/information/astronaut_faq.html#1.

ISS is through Soyuz capsules launched in Russia.

The Risks of Space Exploration

Despite the success of so many space missions, human space exploration is a complex—and often dangerous—pursuit. Each mission relies on the knowledge and skills of hundreds of engineers, astronomers, computer technicians, and mission specialists, even though many of them never communicate directly with one another.

The rockets and spacecraft these people design contain many thousands of complex parts, which increases the risk of an accident. In 1967, Soviet cosmonaut Vladimir Komarov became the first person to die in a space mission when *Soyuz 1* crashed upon its return to Earth. A few years later, three cosmonauts on their way back from Salyut 1 died when their capsule suffered a loss of oxygen and pressure.

The United States maintained a much better safety record than the Soviets during the early years of the Space Race, with the exception of the 1967 *Apollo 1* fire that killed three astronauts on the launch pad. During the 1970s, America scaled back the number of people it sent to space, lowering the chance for disaster. That changed with the space shuttle program, which increased the number of missions—and the odds that something would go wrong.

On January 28, 1986, *Challenger* lifted off on its 10th mission, carrying a satellite payload and a crew that included Christa McAuliffe, a public school teacher who was the first candidate for NASA's Teachers in Space project. As the world watched, the shuttle exploded 73 seconds after liftoff, breaking apart at an altitude of 46,000 feet (14,021 m) and killing all seven crew members. A faulty pressure seal, called an O-ring, in one of the booster rockets caused a fuel leak. The fuel was instantly ignited by the flames erupting from the rocket engines. An investigation was carried out to determine the cause of the defect. The final report, released on June 9, blamed NASA for not having proper safety procedures in place, but it also encouraged the government and public to continue supporting the agency's role in exploration and technical leadership. After the accident, the space shuttle program was

In 2006, this model of Challenger *was unveiled in Christa McAuliffe's hometown of Framingham, Massachusetts, in honor of her and the other astronauts who were killed in the shuttle's explosion.*

grounded until September 29, 1988, and remained accident-free for more than a decade.

This good safety record ended on February 1, 2003, when *Columbia* broke up in the skies over Texas during reentry. All seven crew members were killed. The shuttle had lifted off on its 28th mission on January 16 for a 16-day international scientific program. The next day, NASA personnel examining the launch videos noticed that 81 seconds after liftoff, a piece of foam insulation had broken off the main external fuel tank and struck the shuttle's left wing. It was determined this would not cause a problem during reentry, but it turned out that the foam had also nicked the heat shield. During reentry, hot gases got through the shield, damaging the shuttle so severely that it broke apart. The resulting investigation once again called into question NASA's working culture, and the shuttle program was grounded until July 26, 2005. With problems such as these, it is no surprise that some people are concerned about the dangers of a manned mission to Mars. However, NASA has vowed to improve the safety of its spacecraft to prevent future accidents.

Fortunately, problems sometimes are fixed before they turn deadly. For instance, in September 2018, NASA detected a slight loss of pressure, indicating an air leak, on the ISS while the crew was asleep. It was not enough to put them in danger, so mission control waited until they woke up to have them find the leak. Eventually the astronauts found a small hole in the hull, or outer shell, of the Soyuz capsule that took the astronauts into space. They fixed the hole and the pressure returned to normal, but a mystery remained: What had made the hole?

At first it was believed that the hull had been hit by space debris—or trash—but closer inspection showed the hole had been made by a drill. Roscosmos, the Russian equivalent of NASA, opened an investigation to see whether it was done by accident or on purpose—and if on purpose, why. Had it happened on Earth, while the capsule was being made, or in space, after it docked at the ISS? Political tension between Russia and the United States made the situation more complicated, and news reports gave conflicting information. After some investigation, a Russian website called RIA Novosti reported that the hole was accidentally caused by a worker who helped build the capsule. The worker apparently plugged the hole with glue, which later got sucked out into space.

The Benefits of Space Exploration

Despite the dangers, many people still support space exploration because it has benefited the human race in so many ways. In America and many other industrialized nations, there is a level of convenience and sophistication in life that earlier people did not have. People often take for granted the products and technologies they use every day. Many of these items came about as a result of space exploration.

Satellites play a large role in many of these advancements, and satellite technology has improved greatly since the days of *Sputnik 1* and *Explorer 1*. Since 1957, more than 3,000 satellites have been launched into orbit by more than 50 countries. All of these satellites are identified by their nation of origin, but several have been built and funded by private communications companies. The first was *Telstar 1*, built by AT&T and Bell Telephone Laboratories in 1962.

Early satellite applications in the United States were geared toward military use, but today's satellites serve a variety of purposes beyond just military applications. For example, the use of satellites in public communications has revolutionized society. The idea of communications satellites was first seriously proposed in the modern era by the writer Arthur C. Clarke. In a 1945 magazine article, he described the logistical details of placing objects in fixed orbital positions above Earth to receive signals sent from the ground and then relay them to other geographic points that could not be reached using station-to-station communications on the surface.

Satellites are widely used to help people determine locations. The Global Positioning System (GPS) in the United States, the Galileo positioning system in Europe, and the Compass navigation system in China provide real-time navigational positioning on Earth using several satellites. Millions of people use GPS and similar systems to access maps and get directions, as well as to "check in" to a location on social media. Satellites are also used in entertainment, providing high-quality signals that are much better than what people receive from broadcast systems on the ground.

Most satellites operate for five to fifteen years. After that, their components either break, wear out, or become outdated and must be replaced. According to the United Nations Office for Outer Space Affairs and the Union of Concerned Scientists, there are nearly 5,000 satellites currently in orbit, but fewer than 2,000 are still operating. The non-working satellites sometimes fall to Earth, but most of them continue to fly because there is no cost-effective way to bring them down or collect them in orbit.

Making Life Better with Space Technology

Many products and technologies used on a daily basis also came from the space program. Technologies developed for NASA to use on missions later filtered down to the public. The list of these items is more extensive than most people realize. According to the website Inverse, "Technology from NASA projects has resulted in MRI machines, cell phone cameras, memory foam, and a whole smattering

WHAT GOES UP DOES NOT ALWAYS COME DOWN

It is useful to have working satellites in Earth's orbit, but unfortunately, there is a lot of junk up there too. Millions of pieces of orbital debris, man-made objects that do not serve any purpose, are still floating around. These may be old satellites or spacecraft, but most pieces are fragments of something else and are smaller than a marble. NASA tracks as many pieces as it can to prevent collisions with operational satellites or spacecraft, but some are too small to detect.

With nothing to slow them down, these pieces of debris travel at speeds up to 17,500 miles (28,163 km) per hour. Going that fast, even tiny objects can damage a spacecraft if they collide. In fact, a number of space shuttle windows have required replacing because of damage caused by material that was analyzed and shown to be chips of paint.

In August 2018, American artist Trevor Paglen announced that he would launch a reflective balloon that is 100 feet (30.5 m) long into space. The Orbital Reflector, as it is called, did not have a scientific purpose. Instead, Paglen said it was to encourage "all of us to look up at the night sky with a renewed sense of wonder, to consider our place in the universe, and to reimagine how we live together on this planet."[1] The balloon was intended to fall back to Earth after three months. Some people believed the art project was a worthy goal and approved of it. Others disagreed. They said it was likely that the Orbital Reflector would become another piece of space junk that posed a danger to the ISS.

1. Quoted in Meilan Solly, "Astronomers Say This Reflective Space Sculpture Will Cause Unneeded Light Pollution. The Artist Argues Otherwise," *Smithsonian*, August 24, 2018. www.smithsonianmag.com/smart-news/astronomers-say-trevor-paglens-reflective-space-sculpture-will-generate-unnecessary-light-pollution-artist-argues-otherwise-180970128/.

of safety features in airplanes, which consequently play a fundamental part in supporting the economy down here on earth."[28]

NASA created the Technology Utilization Program (now called the Technology Transfer Program) in 1962 to fulfill its promise to improve life on Earth through its scientific work. The program works to identify NASA technology that might be adapted to use in everyday life. Research into the development of products that are expected to sell well is funded by the program and provided to private companies for a small cost. One of the most important things the program has contributed to is the miniaturization of computer chips, which began out of the necessity of developing smaller and more efficient computers for spacecraft and probes in the 1960s. Smaller computer chips in the private sector led to the development of portable computer devices, cordless power tools, and smaller household appliances.

Items designed and developed for astronaut safety and comfort during missions have also resulted in spinoffs that people on Earth can use. For instance, memory foam, now used in mattresses and pillows, was originally developed for spacecraft seats to lessen the shocks on the body generated during liftoff and reentry. Material used in astronauts' moon boots has been adapted for athletic footwear to provide stability and shock absorption.

NASA technology has also been important in improving public health. Water purification systems developed for long-term space habitation are now used in developing nations to remove harmful bacteria from natural water sources. Computed tomography (CT) and magnetic resonance

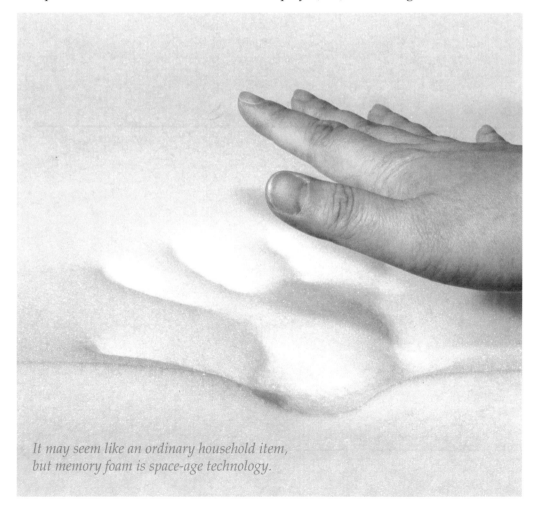

It may seem like an ordinary household item, but memory foam is space-age technology.

imaging (MRI) scans, which are used to diagnose medical conditions, came from computer-enhancement technology developed for studying lunar images.

Changing the Way People View Earth

Space exploration has led to a better quality of life for many people around the world, but it has also given people

a greater understanding of Earth itself, such as its weather and climate systems, its topography, and its wildlife.

NASA's focus on Earth studies began with *TIROS 1*, the world's first Earth-observing satellite, launched in 1960. This satellite provided orbital images of clouds and Earth's weather events, and helped show that Earth's various physical and biological systems

Seeing Hurricane Florence, shown here, from space helped people understand how huge the storm was.

are linked and interactive. *TIROS 1* and later satellites similar to it gathered a large amount of meteorological and atmospheric data, which allowed researchers to develop highly accurate weather forecasting and climate models. These models have done everything from helping farmers with their crops to creating early-warning systems that alert people to devastating storm systems and floods.

It is also helpful to get big-picture photographs of Earth from space. Many astronauts take photos to send back to Earth, and there are cameras on the outside of the ISS as well. On September 14, 2018, NASA astronaut Ricky Arnold took pictures of Hurricane Florence making landfall in North Carolina. His striking photographs showed how large the storm was and could help researchers determine longer-term weather patterns, such as whether hurricanes are getting bigger over time.

The continued collection of atmospheric data has led to an increased understanding of Earth's climate and its changes over time. There is currently an intense debate over how much Earth's climate has been impacted by human behavior, but most scientists agree that in recent decades, the planet has gotten warmer at a rate that is too fast to be explained by natural changes alone. This global warming, researchers say, is causing huge changes to Earth's climate and weather. In the case of Hurricane Florence, for instance, the storm moved more slowly than most hurricanes do. This is dangerous because the longer the storm stays in one place, the more rain and flooding that area will experience. Scientists say a warmer atmosphere is to blame for slow-moving storms. The website Mashable explained,

According to a study in June [2018], hurricanes and typhoons, on average, appear to be slowing down in part because of human-caused climate change. As the climate warms, the way air moves through the atmosphere can become disrupted, possibly blocking these types of storms in place more often. A warming climate also means that the atmosphere can hold more and more water vapor, fueling hurricanes with even more water that can fall on coastal areas.[29]

In recent decades, scientific data collected about Earth's climate has led to some changes in how humans behave. In the 1980s, scientists found a hole in the ozone layer, which protects the planet from the sun's harmful ultraviolet (UV) radiation. That discovery led to a worldwide ban on a number of industrial chemicals that were making the hole larger. Many countries have worked to develop energy-producing technologies that do not rely on fossil fuels such as coal, oil, and natural gas. Burning these fuels creates large amounts of carbon dioxide, which contributes to global warming.

The study of space has also influenced the way people view plants and animals. According to Lisa Ruth Rand, a historian who studies science, technology, and the environment, the pictures of Earth taken from space have changed the way that people think of the planet because people can now see the whole thing at once. She said it made people think, "Not only are we alone in space in this hostile, barren void, but also we are all in it together."[30] Understanding the incredible diversity of life on Earth—and how rare and vulnerable it is—made people more determined to protect it.

LOOKING TO THE FUTURE

Humans have only been around for about 200,000 years, and they have only been able to leave the planet—even temporarily—for the last 70. Considering this, the milestones that have been achieved in space exploration are extraordinary, and it is highly likely that more amazing events await.

Looking Around

The information that astronomers have gathered about the universe in recent years is possible because of a revolution in telescopic imagery. Much of what people know about the way the universe looks is thanks to the Hubble Space Telescope, named after early 20th-century astronomer Edwin Hubble. This device uses visible light to make observations of deep space. It was launched into orbit by the space shuttle *Discovery* on April 24, 1990, after 20 years of development and construction. It gave astronomers much clearer pictures of space than they could get from the ground because the Hubble had no interference from Earth's atmosphere. As NASA explained in 2018, "Outside the haze of our atmosphere, it can see astronomical objects with an angular size of 0.05 arcseconds, which is like seeing a pair of fireflies in Tokyo that are less than 10 feet apart from Washington, D.C."[31]

Hubble's first years in operation were controversial because its performance did not meet expectations. Early images were of poor quality and were out of focus, and designers realized that the device's mirror was the wrong shape. The crew on a 1993 shuttle mission to the Hubble made a series of technical adjustments that improved its quality, and four more missions between 1993 and 2002 made further adjustments to the lenses and upgraded its imaging systems.

Since 1993, high-resolution images collected by Hubble have revealed galaxies billions of light-years away. The

The Hubble Space Telescope, which is about the length of a school bus, has helped improve people's concept of what the universe looks like. It can even take pictures of stars whose light has not yet reached Earth.

telescope has observed the birth and explosion of stars, black holes, and what have come to be known as the Hubble Deep Field and the Hubble Ultra-Deep Field—portions of the sky so far away that they reveal new information about the early period of the universe. The data gathered by Hubble also has led to the discovery of planets orbiting stars in other parts of the Milky Way galaxy, the first of which was discovered in 1995 by Swiss astronomers Michel Mayor and Didier Queloz.

Hubble can no longer be serviced or upgraded since there are no more space shuttle flights, but it is expected to function until the early 2020s. To replace it, other observational tools are already in service or being designed, although some have limitations or have run into complications. The ESA's Herschel Space Observatory, launched on May 14, 2009, has a larger mirror than the Hubble, but it observes only

This impressive image was captured by the Hubble Space Telescope.

in infrared. The James Webb Space Telescope, which NASA is calling the most powerful space telescope in existence, was scheduled for deployment in 2018, but this date was pushed back to 2021 due to several problems. When it does launch, the Webb is intended to be placed farther out than the standard Earth orbit, operating 1 million miles (1.65 million km) away, about four times the distance from Earth to the moon.

Steps Forward, Steps Back

Budget concerns in recent years have affected all aspects of space exploration, from the development of the Webb telescope to NASA's plans for manned spaceflight. In 2010, the last full year of the space shuttle program, launches cost an average of $800 million each. However, the 30-year, $120 billion space shuttle program executed its last launch in July 2011, and many astronomers believed the government did not plan well enough for the continuation of manned flights. On the morning of the last shuttle launch, astrophysicist Neil deGrasse Tyson said, "Apollo in 1969. Shuttle in 1981. Nothing in 2011. Our space program would look awesome to anyone living backwards [through] time."[32]

In 2005, NASA began developing the Constellation program as a replacement for the shuttle program. The goal of Constellation was to pursue scientific activities in space and return humans to the moon for long-term study and the establishment of a semi-permanent lunar base by 2020. This base could be used as a launching pad for missions to Mars and beyond. A new series of rocket boosters was designed and built to launch astronauts and cargo into orbit. Development also began on two spacecraft for Constellation.

President Barack Obama's administration conducted a review of Constellation in 2009. The review concluded that a return to the moon and a human mission to Mars could not be accomplished within the available budget. Concerns for the health and safety of a long-term crew were also considered. For these reasons, Obama canceled funding for the program in 2011.

Other countries continue to move forward. For example, the ESA and Russia's Roscosmos have teamed up for work on the ExoMars project. For this, a Mars rover was scheduled to launch in 2020 to search for signs of life on the planet. The ESA also has indicated a desire to establish an "international moon village," perhaps by the 2030s.

China has been working to improve its rocket launch capabilities for possible future trips to the moon and Mars. Smaller space agencies in countries such as Canada and India are also interested in participating in joint missions.

Space Force

In 2018, President Donald Trump's administration announced plans for a different kind of space project—a military one. Vice President Mike Pence described the details of what the government called a "Space Force." This would be a branch of the U.S. military that would patrol outer space. Pence stated that the government intended to create the Space Force as soon as 2020; according to the *Washington Post*, he "warned of the advancements that potential adversaries are making and issued what amounted to a call to arms to preserve the military's dominance in space."[33]

Opinions about the Space Force have been just as divided as they were over Gingrich's moon base. Again, funding was one concern, but there was also the challenge of government cooperation. Even some people inside the U.S. government have opposed the idea of a Space Force—including the Air Force, since it would lose some of its responsibilities. Without cooperation throughout the government, the already huge task of putting a new military branch into operation would become even harder.

The public has been divided on the issue of whether or not space should be included as a military domain. The 1960s Space Race began as a way to gain military superiority, and even today, the *Washington Post* noted, "Space is vital to the way the United States wages war; the Pentagon's satellites are used for missile defense warnings, guiding precision munitions and providing communications and reconnaissance."[34] Many people think it would

Supporters of a Space Force worry that without it, an enemy nation could destroy American satellites. This would affect the country's communications as well as military equipment. Opponents believe such attacks are unlikely to happen.

be foolish for the United States not to develop a stronger military presence in space, since other countries—including China and Russia—were doing this as of 2018.

Former astronaut Terry Virts, in a 2018 column for the *Washington Post*, argued that many civilians do not understand how important space is to the military. He wrote, "China and Russia … already have access to weapons that threaten our assets in space, either by destroying them in orbit or by crippling ground control through cyberattacks or radio jamming."[35] Virts maintained that a Space Force would be useful if it were given control of satellite launches, developing space equipment, and maintaining land-based defense systems. Some people believe a 21st-century space race would be a good thing, inspiring the types of technological advancements that came in the 20th century, but funded largely by private companies instead of the government.

Other people feel differently. For many people, cost is an important issue. A Space Force would cost billions of dollars. While some private companies might be willing to help pay for the project, it would still require significant government funding—which means tax dollars. Many opponents feel that money could be better spent.

In addition to cost, many people oppose the idea of reinforcing American superiority in outer space. While this was a large part of the national identity in the past, the 21st century has seen a shift in thinking. Some people still believe the United States should keep its position as a world leader in multiple areas, but others believe it is better for countries to work together instead of fighting each other for respect and power. These people would rather see space exploration used as an opportunity for research and to build on what research-based space exploration has already revealed about the universe.

Space Tourism

Some private businessmen and scientists interested in continuing manned spaceflight have teamed up to make commercial space travel a reality. For example, Space Exploration Technologies, also known as SpaceX, was established by PayPal cofounder Elon Musk in 2002. NASA awarded the company a contract in 2006 to develop launchers that can lift commercial payloads into orbit. SpaceX's *Dragon* spacecraft, designed to carry seven astronauts into orbit and beyond, became the first private spacecraft to be successfully launched into orbit and returned to Earth on December 8, 2010.

In addition to professional astronauts, a few tourists have already traveled into space, and many more are excited by the idea. Richard Branson, founder of Virgin Airlines, started the Virgin Galactic Company, which has designed and built spacecraft for low Earth orbit travel in hopes of someday carrying tourists into space. The company's strategy includes using a carrier aircraft to lift a spacecraft, *SpaceShipTwo*, to an altitude of 70,000 feet (21,336 km). *SpaceShipTwo* then would detach and complete the climb to orbit under its own power. *SpaceShipTwo* had completed 15 test flights by 2012, and Branson had hoped to fly complete missions by 2014. Unfortunately, tragedy struck on October 31, 2014. During a test flight, the copilot of the spacecraft changed the position of the tail booms, which are two fin-like attachments on the back of the rocket. When they are in a "feathered" position, they slow the ship down. The copilot feathered the tail booms too soon, causing the rocket to explode. The pilot parachuted to safety, but the copilot died in the crash. Virgin Galactic did not attempt another test flight with active rockets until

Billionaire Elon Musk (inset) started SpaceX, a company that is looking into both space tourism and establishing a permanent colony on Mars.

April 2018. This time, it was successful.

A third company racing to be the first to offer vacations to space is Blue Origin, founded by Amazon CEO Jeff Bezos, who announced that he planned to start selling tickets for about $250,000 each in 2019. Several hundred people rushed to put their names on the list of interested tourists. However, at such a high cost, most people will have to wait a long time before they can afford such a trip.

Which company will win the space tourism race is anyone's guess right now. With its success in 2018, Virgin Galactic put itself in a good position. Blue Origin's test flights also have done well, although it has not done as many—only two as of July 2018—and neither carried passengers, only a dummy named Mannequin Skywalker. In September 2018, news outlets reported that Japanese billionaire Yusaku Maezawa was the first person to sign up for a SpaceX trip around the moon. He put down a deposit on his trip for himself and several others. However, Musk stated that the trip would not take place until 2023 at the earliest.

Some people have criticized these three billionaires for concentrating on space exploration and ignoring problems on Earth that they could contribute money to help solve. Others say that since these men all earned their own money, they can spend it however they want. In the United States, NASA's budget is too small for the agency to do all the work itself. Future space exploration will likely require resources from private investors or other countries.

Humans on Mars

Some people like the idea of leaving the planet for a vacation—and some people are looking for a way to leave it permanently. The astrophysicist Stephen Hawking, who died in 2018, once said, "[Humanity's] only chance for long-term survival is not to remain lurking on planet Earth, but to spread out into space."[36] He pointed out the

THE FIRST SPACE TOURISTS

The first person to ever travel to space as a tourist was American multimillionaire Dennis Anthony Tito. In 2000, Tito paid $20 million for a short stay on the ISS. At first, NASA refused to let him go, but the space tourism company Space Adventures stepped in to help him. He ended up getting a spot on the Soyuz shuttle. According to the Space Adventures website, as of late 2018, the company has arranged eight trips for seven clients—which means one person went twice. Clients also have the option to conduct a spacewalk in the company of a trained astronaut.

environmental problems on the planet, the way humans are quickly using up Earth's natural resources, and the potential for a cosmic disaster such as an asteroid collision as reasons to continue manned space exploration.

Mars, in particular, continues to capture people's imaginations, just as it has for decades. Ray Bradbury's classic science fiction book *The Martian Chronicles*, first published in 1950, contains stories about astronauts landing on Mars and creating a new home for the people of Earth, despite the dangers they find there. It is unlikely that real astronauts would face most of the problems described in Bradbury's book—such as murderous Martians—but creating a colony on Mars would certainly present challenges, especially in the beginning.

The atmosphere on Mars is very similar to Earth's early atmosphere, and its rotation cycle is about the same as Earth's. That gives people hope that it could be terraformed, meaning its environment could be changed into something people could live in. For example, Mars is currently too cold

Theoretically, humans might be able to live on Mars if it was terraformed or if structures were built to support human life.

to support Earth life, so it would have to be warmed up. Some people have suggested doing this by putting huge mirrors in space and pointing them at Mars to reflect more of the sun's light onto the surface of the planet. The website How Stuff Works explained, "The idea would be to concentrate the mirrors on the polar caps to melt the ice and release the carbon dioxide that [is] believed to be trapped inside the ice. Over a period of many years, the rise in temperature would release greenhouse gases."[37] However, NASA scientists do not believe there is enough carbon dioxide on the planet to make this possible. Even if terraforming does eventually work, it would be a huge undertaking. It would require technology beyond what is currently available and would take, at minimum, centuries of work—and probably much longer.

Multiple missions to Mars have been proposed, but so far none have been carried out. In the mid-2000s, many people responded to an advertisement from a company called Mars One, which wanted volunteers to take a one-way trip to Mars and begin establishing a colony as early as 2020. The company held interviews and selected participants, but it did not make much more progress.

In 2014, two students from the Massachusetts Institute of Technology (MIT) published a paper that accused Mars One of making misleading claims about the mission. The students, Sydney Do and Andrew Owens, pointed out that Mars One's first-year budget of $6 billion was far too small for its proposed plans—and that the company did not even have that much money. Do and Owens noted that the first Apollo landing cost NASA $102 billion, and that was for a short walk on the moon's surface. A permanent Mars colony would require not only a spacecraft and the materials to build a colony, but also regular deliveries of necessary items such as food and oxygen. Additionally, the technology Mars One proposed to use did not exist, meaning the company would either have to use a far more expensive spacecraft or change its timeline.

Mars One executives admitted the MIT students were correct but said they hoped to find donors to support the project. As of 2019, that had not happened, but the Mars One website remained active with a revised target date of 2032.

SpaceX

A more realistic Mars mission plan was proposed by Elon Musk's company SpaceX, which stated a goal of sending a mission to Mars in 2022. The SpaceX website stated,

The objectives for the first mission will be to confirm water resources and identify hazards along with putting in place initial power, mining, and life support infrastructure. A second mission, with both cargo and crew, is targeted for 2024, with primary

objectives of building a propellant depot and preparing for future crew flights. The ships from these initial missions will also serve as the beginnings of our first Mars base, from which we can build a thriving city and eventually a self-sustaining civilization on Mars.[38]

In 2017, Musk unveiled a new type of rocket called *BFR* (*Big Falcon Rocket*), which he said could be used for trips on Earth as well as for taking people to Mars. For instance, if people bought a trip from Los Angeles to New York City on *BFR*, some of that money could help pay for the Mars mission. However, as of early 2019, *BFR* was only an idea and not ready to launch. The company's *Falcon Heavy* rocket was much farther along. It completed a successful test launch on February 6, 2018, and deposited a Tesla Roadster car with a dummy driver named Starman in space. As of 2019, the *Falcon Heavy* is the most advanced rocket in existence since the Saturn V.

Many people are excited about the idea of creating a permanent base on Mars. However, others believe the timeline is much longer than Musk and others claim. In 2018, former astronaut Chris Hadfield said of the SpaceX, NASA, and Blue Origin rockets, "My guess is we will never go to Mars with the engines that exist on any of those three rockets unless we truly have to … I don't think those are a practical way to send people to Mars because they're

dangerous and it takes too long."[39] He compared the journey to trying to cross the ocean in a canoe and believes that different forms of propulsion, such as nuclear power instead of liquid fuel, must be developed to address the safety risks. However, these alternate fuel sources are far from being ready to test.

There are other issues as well. Technologically, it is hard enough to return to the moon for a long period of time, let alone travel even farther into space. Money has been a big part of the discussion over whether to continue manned or unmanned space exploration. In 2011, NASA received approximately $19 billion, or 0.5 percent of the total government spending for the year. However, some people believe that the money could be better used to help things such as education or reducing poverty.

With less funding support than it had in the 1960s, NASA must try to develop new, cheaper, safer technology that is powerful enough to send larger rockets with more supplies out of Earth's atmosphere, but this is a difficult goal to achieve.

The Argument Against Plan B

Moving to the moon or Mars is one plan if Earth becomes unlivable, but not everyone thinks this "Plan B" is necessary—or even a good idea. Some think it is dangerous to rely too much on this plan, since it could cause people to see Earth as disposable. In

September 2018, an article published in *Nature* by two conservationists (scientists who try to preserve the environment) suggested that more space on Earth should be reserved for wild plants and animals. However, others argued this would only separate the planet into sections: some for wildlife, others for humans. Astrobiologist Nathalie Cabrol said, "Now we are talking about a bioengineered world, we are not talking about a planet anymore; we are talking about a national park on a planetary level and it's not a biosphere anymore … We are going to create an artificial bubble when what we had was a beautifully working natural system."[40]

This type of artificial biosphere would be necessary on another planet, at least while it was being terraformed, so some people have said that doing it on Earth first would be good practice.

The Biosphere 2 compound (shown here) experienced many problems and showed scientists that humans will face challenges if they try to colonize other worlds.

Others say this is dangerous because if people get it wrong, they risk ruining the only planet they have right now. A project called Biosphere 2 ran from 1991 to 1993 in the Arizona desert. For this experiment, eight people lived in a contained unit designed to be a miniature Earth, but the results were far from successful. According to Space.com writer Meghan Bartels,

It was a troubled experience. One crewmember briefly left the biosphere for emergency medical care. Sweet potatoes thrived so much better than most crops in the high carbon levels that crewmembers' skin picked up a faint orange sheen from eating so many of them. A whopping 40 percent of the species humans had carried with them went extinct.

"It didn't turn out well for a majority of the species—including the humans—that were living there," [science historian Lisa Ruth] Rand said. *"Ultimately, there's a lot of challenges to creating life in microcosm elsewhere, even here."*[41]

Whether people will ever manage to create an artificial, long-term, livable environment remains to be seen. In the meantime, many people believe it is best to focus on ways to live in harmony with the rest of the living things on the planet.

Working Together

Humanity may have a better chance of getting to space if different countries combine their resources and work together. Although space travel was controlled by the United States and Soviet Union in the 1950s and 1960s, the list of nations capable of making spaceflights grew significantly after the establishment of the ESA and its first satellite launch in 1975. Made up of 22 nations, this agency has launched dozens of satellites, deep space probes, and ISS missions since its creation. The Japan Aerospace Exploration Agency (JAXA) was formally established in 2003, but the country has engaged in rocket launches since 1970 that have delivered satellites and scientific payloads into orbit.

These nations have not sent humans into space, but they all have missions to the moon and Mars in various stages of development. As they explore methods of propulsion and spacecraft design, they have pooled their resources with NASA's to share the technological and engineering burdens of future manned space missions.

China is one nation that has not participated heavily in the cooperative effort of space exploration. The country's Communist government keeps its technological advances secret as a matter of policy, much like the former Soviet Union during the Space Race. The Chinese first developed a space

THE GALACTIC PRESIDENT

A man from Nevada named Dennis Hope realized in 1980 that the United Nations (UN) treaty said nothing about individuals owning the moon, so he wrote to the organization to say he was claiming it. The UN never wrote back to tell him he could not, and ever since, he has been selling real estate on the moon to private citizens, including celebrities and several former U.S. presidents. When China announced its intention to build a lunar base, "Hope wrote them a letter saying that their craft would not reach the moon if they didn't have a licensing agreement with him."[1] He compared it to Canada invading the United States and building a structure without government permission. Hope has also declared himself the president of the Galactic Government and the owner of Mercury, Mars, Venus, Pluto, and Jupiter's moon Io.

1. Michael B. Kelley, "The Man Who 'Owns' the Moon Has Made Serious Bank," *Business Insider*, March 26, 2013. www.businessinsider.com/man-selling-real-estate-on-the-moon-2013-3.

program in 1971, but it suffered due to political problems. Despite setbacks, the Chinese did send a manned rocket to space in 2003, joining the United States and Russia as the only countries to have accomplished independent manned missions (as opposed to the cooperative efforts on the ISS). In 2012, China announced its plans to build a manned base on the moon, where it would conduct research, as well as attempt to grow things such as silkworms and flowers. The country did not announce by what year it planned to achieve this goal, but experts say it is likely to be 2030 at the earliest.

If multiple governments and private companies all accomplish their goals of building lunar bases, new questions will arise: To whom does the moon belong? How will it be split? What laws will govern it? The 1967 United Nations Outer Space Treaty states that no single country can own the moon or any other celestial body. It also forbids the countries that have agreed to the treaty from building military installations in space—but who will enforce that treaty if only one or two countries have the ability to go to space?

Some lawyers specialize in space law, which covers national and international laws that govern human activities in space. For example, several private companies have announced their intentions to begin mining asteroids for metals and other materials as early as 2020. A law has already been passed stating that a person is allowed to keep whatever they find on the surface of an asteroid.

However, several areas of space law still need to be clarified. For example, who is responsible if space debris damages a spaceship? Will commercial spaceflight be regulated the way air travel is? These questions and more will need to be answered eventually.

Future Innovations in Space Exploration

Science fiction authors have speculated for decades about what kinds of things might exist in the future, and sometimes the creations of their imaginations have become reality. For example, in 1888, author Edward Bellamy wrote a story in which a man falls asleep in 1887 and wakes up in 2000, where people pay for things using cards instead of cash. Other inventions that have been predicted include video chat, cordless appliances, the Mars rovers, and more.

Science fiction writer Arthur C. Clarke is responsible for more than one of these ideas, as well as for popularizing one that has not come true yet: a space elevator. The idea is to put a satellite into orbit and drop a very long, very strong cable back down to Earth. Materials mined from the moon or asteroids could be transported on the elevator, in addition to people. Although it would initially be expensive, experts say that over time, it would pay for itself through sales of the mined materials. This would make space travel more sustainable, as it would not require a new rocket to be made and

Humans have discovered a lot about space, but it is still only a fraction of what there is to learn.

launched each time. Eventually, it could be affordable enough for the average person to use. Additionally, more than one space elevator could be built.

The reason space elevators have not been built yet is that no material has yet been created that is both strong enough and light enough to make a cable 22,000 miles (35,406 km) long. British scientists Ian Stewart and Jack Cohen, together with fantasy author Terry Pratchett, explained,

The tension in the cable is lowest near the ground, and highest at the top, because each section of cable has to support only the weight of cable below it. So the cable should be made thin at the bottom, and thicker towards the top. The big question is: which material has enough tensile strength? Steel won't do: a steel cable 4 inches (10 cm) wide at the bottom would have to be 2.5 trillion miles (4 trillion km) across at the top ...

For the size to be acceptable, the cable's tensile strength needs to be ... 30 times stronger than steel and 17 times stronger than Kevlar. Such materials do exist: the best known is the carbon nanotube, a molecule of carbon shaped like a hollow cylinder.[42]

Research into carbon nanotubes is ongoing. As of early 2019, however, the longer a nanotube becomes, the weaker it gets. If researchers can perfect the process, a space elevator may become a reality. Partial space elevators that hang in low Earth orbit also have been proposed. They would not have a cable extending to the ground; instead, passengers and cargo would reach them via a balloon or space plane. These would be far less expensive to build and could provide a starting point for a full elevator.

Humanity has made amazing progress in space exploration and learned an incredible amount about the universe in a relatively short period of time. However, there is much more to discover about what is out there, how the universe was formed, and how it affects life on Earth and in outer space. Humans may dream of space travel, but much more research needs to be done before that could ever become a part of life for the average person. Until then, most people will have to admire the cosmos the old-fashioned way: by looking up at the stars.

Notes

Introduction:
The Final Frontier

1. Taylor Casti, "Ocean vs. Space: Which Is the True Final Frontier?," Mashable, September 25, 2013. mashable.com/2013/09/25/ocean-vs-space/#xav16JJAcgqg.

2. Megan Wilde, "Galileo's Telescope," The Galileo Project, accessed on August 20, 2018. galileo.rice.edu/bio/narrative_6.html.

Chapter One:
Discovering the Universe

3. Quoted in Bill Bryson, *A Short History of Nearly Everything*. New York, NY: Broadway Books, 2003, e-book.

4. John Noble Wilford, ed. *Cosmic Dispatches: The* New York Times *Reports on Astronomy and Cosmology*. New York, NY: Norton, 2001, p. 222.

5. Jimmy Stamp, "The History of Rocket Science," *Smithsonian*, February 2013. www.smithsonianmag.com/innovation/the-history-of-rocket-science-4078981.

6. "Konstantin E. Tsiolkovsky," NASA, September 22, 2010. www.nasa.gov/audience/foreducators/rocketry/home/konstantin-tsiolkovsky.html.

Chapter Two:
The Race to the Moon

7. Quoted in David Halberstam, *The Fifties*. New York, NY: Villard, 1993, p. 623.

8. The Editors of *Encyclopedia Britannica*, "Katherine Johnson," *Encyclopedia Britannica*, last updated August 22, 2018. www.britannica.com/biography/Katherine-Johnson-mathematician.

9. Quoted in Alan Shepard and Deke Slayton, *Moon Shot: The Inside Story of America's Space Race*. Atlanta, GA: Turner, 1994, p. 35.

10. Quoted in Robert A. Caro. *The Years of Lyndon Johnson: Master of the Senate.* New York, NY: Knopf, 2002, p. 1028.

11. The Editors of *Encyclopedia Britannica*, "Margaret Hamilton," *Encyclopedia Britannica*, last updated August 13, 2018. www.britannica.com/biography/Margaret-Hamilton-American-computer-scientist.

12. Deborah Cadbury, *Space Race: The Epic Battle Between America and the Soviet Union for Dominion of Space.* New York, NY: HarperCollins, 2006, p. 180.

13. Quoted in Hans Mark, ed., *The Encyclopedia of Space Science and Technology, Volume 1.* Hoboken, NJ: Wiley, 2003, p. 702.

14. Quoted in Neil deGrasse Tyson, "The Case for Space: Why We Should Keep Reaching for the Stars," *Foreign Affairs*, March/April 2012, p. 23.

15. Chris Kraft, *Flight: My Life in Mission Control.* New York, NY: Penguin, 2001, p. 352.

16. Quoted in Erik Bruun and Jay Crosby, eds., *Our Nation's Archives: The History of the United States in Documents.* New York, NY: Black Dog & Leventhal, 1999, p. 780.

17. Quoted in Ivan D. Ertel, Roland W. Newkirk, and Courtney G. Brooks, *The Apollo Spacecraft: A Chronology, Volume IV.* Washington, DC: NASA History Program Office, 1978, part 3, (E).

18. Stuart Miller, "Newt Gingrich Promises Moon Base by the End of His Second Term," *Guardian*, January 25, 2012. www.theguardian.com/world/blog/2012/jan/25/newt-gingrich-moon-base.

19. N.L., "The Pros and Cons of Moon Base Gingrich," *The Economist*, January 30, 2012. www.economist.com/democracy-in-america/2012/01/30/the-pros-and-cons-of-moon-base-gingrich.

Chapter Three:
Unmanned Missions and the Search for Life

20. R. Cargill Hall, *Lunar Impact: A History of Project Ranger.* Washington, DC: NASA History Program Office, 1977, p. 309.

21. Carl Sagan, *Cosmos.* New York, NY: Random House, Inc., 1980, p. 94.

22. Elizabeth Howell, "Pioneer 10: Greetings from Earth," Space.com, September 18, 2012. www.space.com/17651-pioneer-10.html.

23. Sagan, *Cosmos*, p. 287.

24. "Mission to Saturn: Cassini-Huygens," Jet Propulsion Laboratory, accessed on August 28, 2018. www.jpl.nasa.gov/missions/cassini-huygens.

25. Bryson, *A Short History of Nearly Everything*.

Chapter Four:
Further Exploration

26. Marina Koren, "What the Heck Happened on the International Space Station?," *The Atlantic*, September 8, 2018. www.theatlantic.com/science/archive/2018/09/international-space-station-nasa-russia-leak/569692/.

27. Michael Koziol, "10 Disgusting Ways Your Body Betrays You in Space," *Popular Science*, November 3, 2016. www.popsci.com/how-your-body-betrays-you-in-space.

28. Hannah Margaret Allen, "How NASA Makes Money, Contributes to the United States Economy," Inverse, February 18, 2018. www.inverse.com/article/39318-nasa-budget-contribute-to-the-us-economy.

29. Miriam Kramer, "NASA Video Shows Massive Scale of Hurricane Florence from Space," Mashable, September 14, 2018. mashable.com/article/nasa-video-hurricane-florence-from-space/#edSnKzHJJZqx.

30. Quoted in Meghan Bartels, "How Space Exploration Can Teach Us to Preserve All Life on Earth," Space.com, September 13, 2018. www.space.com/41818-earth-biodiversity-conservation-lessons-from-space.html.

Epilogue:
Looking to the Future

31. "About the Hubble Space Telescope," NASA, last updated March 6, 2018. www.nasa.gov/mission_pages/hubble/story/index.html.

32. Neil deGrasse Tyson, "Back to the Final Frontier," *Discover*, April 2012, p. 56.

33. Christian Davenport and Dan Lamothe, "Pence Details Plan for Creation of Space Force in What Would Be the Sixth Branch of the Military," *Washington Post*, August 9, 2018. www.washingtonpost.com/business/economy/pence-details-plan-for-creation-of-space-force-in-what-would-be-the-sixth-branch-of-the-military/2018/08/09/0b40b8d0-9bdc-11e8-8d5e-c6c594024954_story.html?noredirect=on&utm_term=.2f6d5f7dd251.

34. Davenport and Lamothe, "Pence Details Plan for Creation of Space Force."

35. Terry Virts, "I Was an Astronaut. We Need a Space Force," *Washington Post*, August 23, 2018. www.washingtonpost.com/opinions/i-was-an-astronaut-we-need-a-space-force/2018/08/23/637667e6-a6fb-11e8-b76b-d513a40042f6_story.html?utm_term=.4e84bddf5a2c.

36. Quoted in Cassandra Szklarski, "Stephen Hawking: Space Exploration Crucial to Human Survival," *Huffington Post*, November 18, 2011. www.huffingtonpost.ca/2011/11/18/stephen-hawking-space-exploration_n_1101975.html.

37. Kevin Bonsor, "How Terraforming Mars Will Work," How Stuff Works, November 6, 2000. science.howstuffworks.com/terraforming2.htm.

38. "Missions to Mars," SpaceX, accessed on August 29, 2018. www.spacex.com/mars.

39. Quoted in David Z. Morris, "This Retired Astronaut Says SpaceX and NASA Rockets 'Will Never Go to Mars,'" *Fortune*, June 17, 2018. fortune.com/2018/06/17/chris-hadfield-nasa-spacex-mars.

40. Quoted in Bartels, "How Space Exploration Can Teach Us."

41. Quoted in Bartels, "How Space Exploration Can Teach Us."

42. Terry Pratchett, Ian Stewart, and Jack Cohen, *The Science of Discworld*. New York, NY: Anchor Books, 2002, e-book.

For More Information

Books

Bryson, Bill. *A Short History of Nearly Everything*. New York, NY: Broadway Books, 2003.
> This book discusses scientific achievements and discoveries, including ones that relate to space, in plain language.

Jackson, Libby. *Galaxy Girls: 50 Amazing Stories of Women in Space*. New York, NY: Harper Design, 2018.
> Women who have contributed to space exploration, including Katherine Johnson, Sally Ride, and Peggy Whitson, are the subject of this book.

Kruesi, Liz. *Space Exploration*. Minneapolis, MN: Essential Library, 2016.
> The author discusses some of the most interesting current cosmic studies.

Launius, Roger D., and Andrew K. Johnston. *Smithsonian Atlas of Space Exploration*. New York, NY: HarperCollins, 2009.
> This book contains an extensive visual history of space exploration, including information from the Smithsonian Air and Space Museum collection.

Stefoff, Rebecca. *Space Race: An Interactive Space Exploration Adventure*. North Mankato, MN: Capstone Press, 2017.
> The reader gets to choose the direction of this book. Each choice they make determines which historical details are revealed to them.

Tyson, Neil deGrasse. *Space Chronicles: Facing the Ultimate Frontier*. New York, NY: Norton, 2012.
> Tyson, through a series of essays, defines the importance of continued space exploration for knowledge as well as for America's economy and security.

Websites

BrainPop

www.brainpop.com

Searching the word "space" on this website allows users to read articles and play games to learn more about space exploration of the past and present.

Exoplanet Exploration

exoplanets.nasa.gov

This website, which is run by NASA's Astrophysics Division, describes the search for other planets that can sustain human life.

Hubblesite

hubblesite.org

Visitors to this website can learn about the constellations and see pictures of what the Hubble telescope has seen in the past, as well as what it is viewing at the current moment.

NASA

www.nasa.gov

The official website for the National Aeronautics and Space Administration includes updated information on its latest missions, projects, and responsibilities.

Space Scoop

www.spacescoop.org/en

This internet news website focuses exclusively on space exploration, science, astronomy, and technology. It also includes games and activities.

Index

Picture Credits

About the Author

Jennifer Lombardo earned her BA in English from the University at Buffalo and still resides in Buffalo, New York, with her cat, Chip. She has helped write a number of books for young adults on topics ranging from world history to body image. In her spare time, she enjoys cross-stitching, hiking, and volunteering with Habitat for Humanity.